What a wonderful col [illegible]
phetic insights my d [illegible] shares in this
new book. Not only will you be encouraged but you will be inspired as the Holy Spirit opens your eyes to the supernatural power of God.

—Joni Lamb
Cofounder, Daystar Television Network

Hubie Synn is a dear friend with a powerful prophetic gift that has helped transform many lives. His first book told the story of his beginnings, and this second book continues to relate his amazing journey. If you want to be inspired to be used of God powerfully, this book is a must-read!

—Bishop Joseph Mattera
Founder, Christ Covenant Coalition;
Overseeing Bishop, Resurrection Church

My friend Hubie shares in a way that demystifies the prophetic. He takes the spookiness out of it and reveals the loving, compassionate God who has incredible plans for us. He is truly a wandering prophet carrying a heavenly treasure in his earthen vessel.

—Bishop Dale C. Bronner
Founder and Senior Pastor, Word of Faith Family
Worship Cathedral

The voice of God is as multifaceted as God is, thus the need for a variety of prophets and prophetic ministers to communicate the breadth of His voice on the earth. Hubie Synn is a beautiful human being and a passionate lover of God who is being used powerfully by the Lord to represent His voice in the earth today. Hubie's testimony gives so many people across the body of Christ the courage to embrace the unique way God has created them in their personalities, physical makeup, and vocational settings. One of the keys I see in this book is the power of saying yes to becoming a vessel of the Lord's love and a voice of God no matter where we find ourselves. The other thing that stood out was how much God loves people and wants to intersect their lives with His voice so they will become aware of His love. I hope and trust you will enjoy this book as much as I did.

—David Balestri
National Convener, Australian Coalition of Apostolic Leaders

Hubie Synn's new book, *Lessons From a Wandering Prophet*, provides a welcome and insightful sequel to his first book, *The Tales of a Wandering Prophet*. As the title implies, the book chronicles lessons relating to prophecy the author learned through a series of divine appointments with an eclectic array of persons, many of whom were previously unknown to him.

My wife, Alaine, and I were among these anonymous strangers to receive a word from Hubie. Since our first memorable encounter in Dallas, we can testify how God has used Hubie to bring powerful and accurate prophetic words to a diverse collection of men and women in our nation of Australia.

Hubie Synn is a man with a passion to see authentic personal prophecy released in the earth. He skillfully takes us through numerous relational scenarios, each containing cogent lessons designed to raise the bar of prophetic ministry in the current season.

—Dr. John McElroy
Founder and Director, Southern Cross Association of Churches

Lessons From a Wandering Prophet is definitely a must-read for all seekers who love Jesus and desire to be led by the Holy Spirit. Hubie Synn's multiple gifts as an entrepreneur and a prophet who is apostolic makes for an interesting, revelational, and relevant book. It's one of the most enjoyable books I have read in a long time!

—John P. Kelly
Founder and Convening Apostle,
International Coalition of Apostolic Leaders

I have had the privilege of knowing Hubie Synn for the last nine years as a co-laborer in the work of ministry but more importantly as a friend. His journey of walking in his prophetic calling is refreshing and eye-opening. Hubie's life is a testament that God can use any of us in any way if we make ourselves available. In *Lessons From a Wandering Prophet*, Hubie shares his personal journey through the process and schooling through which the Holy Spirit takes every person He chooses to use.

I have experienced Hubie's prophetic gift in my own life and ministry. I discovered it to be accurate and encouraging. His integrity, humility, and down-to-earth delivery of his gift distinguish his ministry of the prophetic as extremely practical and impactful. As you read this book, you will see that God still uses normal people to do His work on the earth. You will also be invited to participate in learning how to speak for God in a way that brings glory to Him!

—Rev. Walter E. Nistorenko
Lead Pastor, Abundant Life Church

Hubie Synn has lived a very disciplined prophetic life for many years. His prophetic gift is undeniable. He understands what it takes to stay grounded in both his spirituality and his humanity as a prophetic voice for this generation.

Hubie's book *Lessons From a Wandering Prophet* will help those who desire to use their prophetic gift and live a life that honors the gift they possess. Knowing how to balance discipleship and leadership is a gift to the body of Christ that should be embraced and emulated.

—Rev. Courtney Wright
Chief Pastoral Support Officer,
Christian Alliance of Pastors

Hubie Synn is not just anointed but is one of the sincerest and humblest people I have ever had the pleasure of calling my friend. Those who sit in the office of a prophet often can be quite aggressive; however, Hubie possesses a deep gentleness and is unapologetic about what the Lord is doing.

He cares very little about what man thinks and instead focuses on pleasing the Lord. That is an exceedingly rare and beautiful quality to have in the days we live in.

This book will inspire many and help people understand their journey and the process God brings us all through to cause us to walk in His destiny. It has been a pleasure to read, and I am enriched because of it.

—Marsha Mansour
Revivalist, Ordained Assemblies of God Minister

As many will attest, Hubie Synn is the real deal. In a world that craves authenticity, he is an authentic person with an extraordinary gift.

This is an important book because it displays the heart of a dear friend who has surrendered his life and gifts to God. But it is also a practical book, addressing how to live day by day with the wonderful and challenging reality that God is moving in these mortal tents. Be open and prepared to stretch a bit, and this book will bless you greatly.

—Joseph Infranco
Pastor and Constitutional Attorney

Lessons From a Wandering Prophet is a powerfully simple yet supernaturally profound reminder of what life can and ought to be when we say yes to God and allow His wisdom, discernment, loving-kindness, correction, and direction to navigate our lives. Throughout each chapter, the reader is invited to a front-row seat of the Synn family's journey and the lessons, blessings, and losses they have experienced to the glory of God. In this regard, the book provides major keys of wisdom on how to shepherd as well as protect oneself and those you love from the demands of full-time ministry.

—Pastors Andrew "Mo" Jr. and
Dr. Kendra A. Momon
Lead Pastors, Victory World Church,
Midtown Atlanta

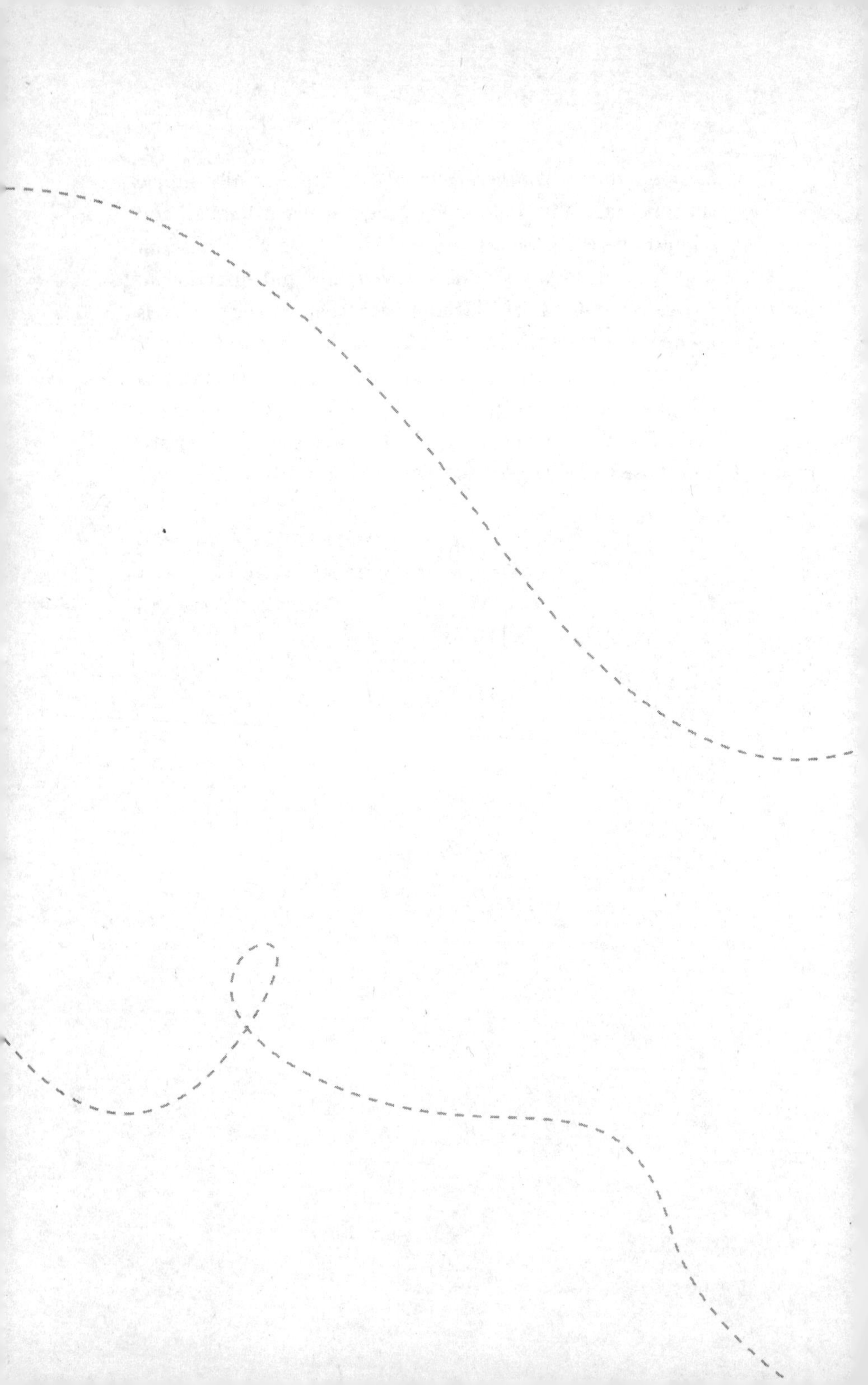

LESSONS FROM A *Wandering* PROPHET

HUBIE SYNN

Most Charisma Media products are available at special quantity discounts for bulk purchase for sales promotions, premiums, fund-raising, and educational needs. For details, call us at (407) 333-0600 or visit our website at www.charismamedia.com.

Lessons From a Wandering Prophet by Hubie Synn
Published by Charisma House, an imprint of Charisma Media
600 Rinehart Road, Lake Mary, Florida 32746

Visit the author's website at www.hubiesynn.com.

Cataloging-in-Publication Data is on file with the Library of Congress.
International Standard Book Number: 978-1-63641-118-7
E-book ISBN: 978-1-63641-119-4

22 23 24 25 26 — 987654321
Printed in the United States of America

Contents

Acknowledgments

THE FOLLOWING PEOPLE have shaped my life throughout the years, and I can't thank them enough!

To Vicki, my better half and cowriter—we have had an interesting journey, and I never would have gotten to this point without you. Thank you for standing beside me at all times!

To my children, Sara, Daniel, Krissy, Paul, and Michael—I love you more than you could possibly know and am so proud of each of you. Each one of you is different, and that makes it such a joy to be your dad. Thank you for being all I could ever ask for!

I would like to thank the following people, who have walked with me through the journey to writing this book: Steve and Joy, Debbie, Adrienne, Prudence and Eric, Dot, Richard and Nora, Rena, Rachelle, Kathie Lee, SQuire and Louise (SQuise), Woodley, Elise and Michael, Helen, Marsha, Danyale, Dr. Sheena, Rupesh, Baird, Augusta, Max, Margie,

Kimberly, Judy, Glacia and Emerson, Laura, Margaret, Alice and Asher, Cherry, Danny, John Kelly, Daryn, Patty, Anne, Luca, Jet, and Storm.

I also would like to thank the following families: the Cahns, Lambs, Bakkers, Matteras, Sepes, Shahids, Rathanums, Crosslands, Vincents, McCormicks, Correas, DaCuhnas, Nistorenkos, Merlinos, Schweisthals, Onyias, Ahluwalias, Raises, Rifkins, Jamisons, Rands, Chois, Moels, Neals, Barbaricks, Lees, Shirleys, Dashers, Elharfouches, Mansours, Sullivans, Kartsakalis, Morantes, Shins, McLemores, Landaverdes, Loihles, Ramers, Colletons, Sobels, Dugans, Balestris, McElroys, Johnstons, Momons, Cavas, Wilsons, and Infrancos.

Foreword

I HAVE MET SO many fascinating people during my decades on planet earth. Several of them have stood out as truly special.

Hubie Synn is one of them. He is a self-described "wandering prophet," but to me he is more of a reluctant prophet, like Jonah in the Bible, who refused to obey God's commandment to take His message of salvation to the people of Nineveh.

Now, Hubie doesn't refuse to obey God when he gets a word from Him, but he gets literally sick to his stomach when the Lord is prompting him to prophesy. I understand his reluctance, though I'm certainly no prophet of God. We're human, and there are times in all our lives when we say, "Really, Lord? You want me to do *what*?"

I love Hubie's humanity, his humility, and his self-deprecating humor. Because Hubie is an accountant from New Jersey, on the surface he's an ordinary guy. But in spiritual realms Hubie is a deeply committed, serious student of the Word and a true prophet of God.

I have been blessed to call Hubie a dear friend for years now, and I have seen his life and ministry up close and personal.

I love him for so many reasons, and I'd be happy to list them for you, but it's much better if you discover them for yourself, as you will when you read this book you're now holding.

I pray that you will open your mind to the gifts of the Spirit as described in the Bible in 1 Corinthians 12:8–10. And I pray that you will open your heart to this amazing servant of God and the message he has for you.

Shalom!

—Kathie Lee Gifford

Introduction

As I have grown in my walk with the Lord and in the prophetic ministry He has entrusted to me, I have had many adventures and learned significant lessons along the way. My first book, *The Tales of a Wandering Prophet*, detailed how I literally fell into prophetic ministry over twenty years ago when the Holy Spirit started orchestrating divine meetings for me to prophesy to people from all walks of life in locations and venues mainly outside the church setting. My life really changed when He led me to prophesy to David Tyree, an NFL wide receiver, and Jonathan Cahn, author of *The Harbinger*, and the fulfillment of those prophecies was publicized. Although I do not have any formal training in prophetic ministry, I soon discovered that recognizing and being obedient to the voice of the Holy Spirit allowed Him to quickly move me forward in my prophetic gift. In doing this, God proved that He can use ordinary individuals for His glory.

This book, *Lessons From a Wandering Prophet*, continues the story of what happened to me and my family after the prophetic gift changed our lives and we grew deeper in our relationships with God and one another. Issues arose in the ministry and our personal lives that we did not anticipate, but the Lord used them to bring healing in our lives and release my prophetic gift to a new level. This book describes the questions, concerns, and situations that arose regarding the handling of the prophetic gift and our personal relationships and the principles God taught us to apply to these situations. I've used these same principles to help many believers who are called to prophetic ministry, as well as those called to other types of ministry.

No matter what area of ministry we are called to serve in, the Lord wants to use all of us to make a difference, so I wrote *Lessons From a Wandering Prophet* as a simple, practical handbook and source of encouragement to everyday believers. Ministry can be wildly fruitful and gratifying when you see lives being changed and people's spirits being awakened, but it comes with challenges. My prayer is that as I share my experiences and the principles the Lord has taught me personally, you will be equipped with the keys to overcoming similar challenges so your spiritual gifts can be released to the next level.

And of some have compassion, making a difference.

—Jude 22, kjv

Chapter 1

Divinely Positioned

IT WAS A typical day at the height of another tax season. I had been working around the clock for three months, and the push was on for the finish line. Of course, that's when all the procrastinators started sending their tax information in dribs and drabs at the last moment, adding more fuel to the fire of the looming deadlines. My sore eyes were strained, and my head was hurting, so I decided to take a short break to clear my mind. Needing a momentary distraction from the growing piles of work on my desk, I decided to check my Facebook messages. Scrolling through the long list, I noticed a message from a stranger named SQuire Rushnell, and I felt led to open it.

His brief introduction mentioned that he was the author of the Godwink book series and he would like to interview me for his upcoming book, *The 40 Day Prayer Challenge*. SQuire went on to describe it as "an extension of the Divine Alignment thesis…the mysterious connections which cause us to be in the right place at the right time to encounter the very person who can help us do what God has in mind for us to do."[1]

"Hmm," I thought. "Interesting book title and subject." In addition, I noticed that SQuire had a monthly "Godwink" feature on NBC's *Today With Kathie Lee & Hoda*. He appeared legitimate, and at this point I didn't have discernment to stop reading the message or accept his offer, so I knew I needed to pray more about it before responding. I'm always humbled and honored when someone wants to interview me, but I'm also cautious because I receive numerous requests and need discernment as to which ones the Lord wants me to accept. Besides, my five-minute break was up, and I needed to get back to work because time was ticking toward my deadlines.

Later the same day, SQuire left me another message, elaborating on the theme of his book series, which focuses on God's alignment and positioning, kind of like God's GPS. Now my interest was piqued because that has kind of been the story of my prophetic ministry life since it started. While exploring the Godwinks website, I began to reflect on how the Lord had put me in places at certain times for divine appointments that brought alignment into people's lives through the prophetic.

I witnessed both ordinary and amazing encounters such as the ones that led to the prophecies behind David Tyree's miraculous catch for the New York Giants during the 2008 national football championship and "the miracle at the airport" that confirmed God's plans for Jonathan Cahn's book *The Harbinger*, which became a *New York Times* best seller, and led to his connecting with the company that ultimately would publish it. You can read about these in my previous book, *The Tales of a Wandering Prophet*. To this day I still cannot believe God led me to be part of those moments. Maybe the Lord was up to something here with this Godwinks guy, but I was in no rush to respond, especially during this final tax season push. Every minute I spend ministering to someone is time I'll have to make up by working into the early hours of the morning.

Four days later, however, after a prompting from the Holy Spirit, I responded to SQuire's messages and agreed to squeeze in the follow-up phone call he requested. I had to drive to Queens, New York, the following day to see a client and would be in the car for at least an hour, so we scheduled our call for then. Because God has surprised me so many times, I've learned to be pliable and open to the movement of the Holy Spirit, even when it comes in unexpected ways and at seemingly inconvenient times. I go about my routine, and for me that means praying in the Spirit throughout the day to stay sensitive to the Lord's voice. As I do this, He frequently uses something that happens, some circumstance, to interrupt me and bring me to someone, or bring someone to me, and then gives me a prophetic word to deliver to the person.

I try to stay grounded because if the Lord is bringing an assignment to me, then it is to accomplish His will and purposes; it's not about me. My role is simply to be obedient. I've been on assignment enough times to know I can trust God to redeem the time and help me finish my work no matter how close I am to the midnight deadline. There are times when I barely make the deadline, but I always seem to have a few seconds to spare. I firmly believe that if we take care of God's business, He will always take care of ours. Jesus said, "But seek first the kingdom of God and His righteousness, and all these things shall be added to you" (Matt. 6:33).

While I was stuck in heavy traffic on the New Jersey Turnpike, SQuire called, and we started to chat. It was a pleasant surprise when his wife, Louise, joined us on the phone to chime in on the discussion. Within minutes it became obvious that they had mutual respect and valued each other's input. This was refreshing because in so many of the exchanges I've had with couples, the husband dominates while the wife stays quiet in the background.

"I was the vice president of family programming at ABC and helped to create the *Schoolhouse Rock!* series and *Afterschool Specials*," SQuire said. The moment he mentioned *Schoolhouse Rock!*, an excitement leaped to life inside me, and I began to recall those songs from my childhood. I loved that series! Even today, many decades later, I still remember the lyrics to "Conjunction Junction." I watched *Schoolhouse Rock!* almost every Saturday morning.

Then Louise mentioned that she'd been a regular on *The Hollywood Squares* game show, which I also grew up loving. Suddenly the call took a new turn, and I was thrilled at the opportunity to meet these two. Instead of feeling frustrated with the bumper-to-bumper traffic, I was happy to have this uninterrupted time to talk to them.

Louise explained that she had stumbled across my story on the *Divine Intervention* internet radio show and then spoken to SQuire about it. They both decided to reach out to me to set up a formal interview for me to tell my story for their upcoming book. At this point, I had a peace about talking with them. As we chatted a bit more and began wrapping up the call, I felt a familiar nudge. "Uh-oh," I thought. But before I could consider all the reasons not to say something, I heard myself say, "You can't go yet!" Then another thought popped into my head: "If this goes badly, there goes my interview." Before more anxious thoughts could fill my mind, Louise said, "Why?"

"Because the Lord wants to tell you both something," I said, the words coming out of my mouth as if they had had a mind of their own.

Then it started.

"The Lord wants to speak to Louise first and then to SQuire," I said. All this was happening while I was trying to focus on the road, so it seemed like a blur. I am not sure how long I spoke to them, but when I finished, there was a moment of silence on the other end of the phone. I could feel my heart pounding against my chest. A silence or pause from the person receiving the prophetic word is always scary to me, especially if I am speaking with someone by phone. Then the sound of laughter erupted through the speaker. I wasn't sure if SQuire and Louise were laughing at me or were joyful. Either way, I was nervous until Louise said, "Amazing."

"Whew." I breathed a sigh of relief.

When we're moving in the prophetic, sometimes the Holy Spirit is dictating so fast that we do not know what we are saying. This can be difficult, so insecurities can and will flare up. Yet if we are living a life of obedience, we can trust God to bring us through it. He can even work out mistakes for His and our good. The key is to die to self and be a willing vessel.

The prophetic word was amazing to them because it spoke about some specific issues they were facing at that time. It also addressed situations from their past and things that were coming. It met them where they were, reminding them of their past to show how the Lord was with them and knew all the details of their lives and then giving them hope of what was to come. All this was spoken at our initial meeting, so I could not have known any of it. Thankfully, since the word was accurate, they still wanted me to do the book interview, which we set up later.

When SQuire and Louise contacted me that first time, I was simply living my life, doing what I do. God was the One who brought them to me. I didn't have to do anything but be available and in tune with Him. I was not looking for an opportunity to put my name out there. Promotion, advancement, and assignments for His purposes come from Him. We just need to be available. If we are yielded to Him, then He will orchestrate the way to move us forward in that which He has for us. If God has called us, we don't need to look for opportunities or knock down doors; He will present them to us. Our responsibility is to be prepared and ready at all times to do what He wants us to do.

I was talking to my friend Pastor Dan Correa at lunch recently. He said, "The one thing I've learned from you over the years, Hubie, is you don't do anything." He continued, "You just sit there, live your life, and whenever it [the prophetic unction] springs up, you're obedient to the call. And then if there's no call, you don't do anything and are content. It is just amazing to see what the Lord does with you and the doors He opens for you!"

His words are humbling, but Pastor Dan is right. Since the beginning of my prophetic journey with God, I have never promoted myself in any way or pursued networking to secure speaking engagements, book contracts, or any other opportunity, and I do not plan to. For example, I was asked to write this book and prayed to see if it was a God opportunity. Not all opportunities are of God even if they may *seem* good. We are operating under circumstantial faith when we assume every opportunity that appears must be from the Lord.

I have lived like this in the past and know firsthand the consequences of this way of thinking. I have also witnessed the negative outcomes friends have experienced when they've done this. There is a big difference between God directing your path and your taking a path because it shows up. Learning to discern the difference is the key. Having the courage to say no can often keep us in divine alignment, which will protect us from setbacks and delays in what God has in store for us.

Learning to Discern

There are a few important lessons regarding discernment that I have learned on my prophetic journey. Getting a check in our spirit could mean different things. It could mean no or caution or keep your guard up. A check in our spirit is like the Holy Spirit's warning. When it goes on, we should proceed but with caution. If we choose to ignore it, then there could be consequences. This is why it is critical to be sensitive to the Holy Spirit's voice and obey. Forging full steam ahead when our warning light is on can lead to issues, even if we have good intentions.

Paul and Silas wanted to preach the gospel in a certain part of Asia, which seemed like a good thing. Aren't we supposed to preach the gospel everywhere? Yet the Bible says, "They were forbidden by the Holy Spirit to preach the word in Asia" (Acts 16:6). The Lord knew something Paul and Silas didn't. The same is true for us. The Holy Spirit knows all things, and sometimes He will forbid us or give us warnings. For this reason, discernment is essential when moving in the prophetic. Let's look at a couple of ways we can discern.

One kind of discernment is when the Lord is letting you know to stay away. My mentor Jack Forde taught me about this. I typically get a very strong, uneasy feeling, kind of like I'm being pushed or red sirens are going off. You may not know why you feel uneasy; you just know something isn't right, and you can't shake the warning deep inside your head and/or heart.

There is also a kind of discernment that is telling us to proceed with caution. When this happens to me, I tend to feel that it may be OK to proceed, but there is some uneasiness. At this point, I am not sure why I feel uneasy, so I just keep my guard up and move forward. In situations like these, you step out in a situation and see how it develops, and additional discernment and direction from the Holy Spirit kick in later. When you eventually begin to sense the Lord's discernment and direction, you start to slow things down to see what He is telling you. You still don't know everything as you walk it out, but you are confident the Holy Spirit is guiding you and knows what He's doing. It's like the time Jesus told Peter, "You do not understand now what I am doing but you will later" (John 13:7, NLV).

One day I received an email from a reality television show producer. Ironically she had come across my name in *The 40 Day Prayer Challenge*, the book SQuire and Louise interviewed me for, and she wanted to discuss making a reality television show focused on my family and my prophetic gift. My first thought was, "Really? Us? Is this for real?" So I went online and researched the woman to see if she was legitimate. I also emailed SQuire and Louise, who have a history in the television industry, to get their advice and ask for their prayers.

While I was waiting for their response, I told my wife, Vicki, and our five children about the email. Some of the children were excited and some were lukewarm about the possibility of being on television. But the more I thought about possibly doing a show, the more the idea began to grow on me. "I could be a reality star," I thought. "We could have our own show. We wouldn't have to be concerned about college costs. Vicki and I could possibly quit our jobs."

As the day went on, I got more and more excited about the possibilities; then suddenly it hit me that I had neglected to do the one thing I always do: pray. I paused for a moment and asked God for forgiveness because I completely forgot to include Him and basically let my thoughts get carried away. I asked God if I should move forward, and I did not get any uneasiness or uncomfortable feelings. This is usually a sign from God that it is OK to proceed. I responded to the producer, and we set up a time for me to meet with her and her husband in New York City for lunch. "It can't hurt," I thought, "and I don't have any red sirens warning me not to do it."

So I met with this couple, and we chatted all through lunch about the possible show and the logistics of how it would work. While we were eating, the conversation switched to the prophetic gift. They were keenly interested in where the gift has taken me and what was currently happening. As we were chatting, I felt that familiar nudge.

"Can it wait, God?" I asked silently. "We are discussing a possible show, and if I blow it here, then it will never happen." Negative thoughts filled my mind about giving a prophetic word and it possibly being wrong. Then I started to feel sick to my stomach, so I said, "Excuse me. I need to use the restroom." I started to pray under my breath as I got up from my chair and made my way to the restroom. In the restroom I submitted to the Lord, and my stomach calmed down. I made my way back to my seat and told them, "I want to pray for you both."

"OK!" they eagerly nodded.

As soon as they said, "OK," the words came flying out. I could tell they were listening closely, and then they both started to smile. "That was incredible," the producer said, and her husband agreed. We chatted some more about the show, and they ended the meeting by saying they would send a contract for me to review.

During the drive home I tried to process what had just taken place, because it seemed surreal. Were we really getting a television show? What would that be like? How would the kids handle being on-screen and people recognizing them? As I started to consider all these questions, an uneasiness came over me. I wasn't exactly sure what it was or meant, but my guard was now up. As time passed, the uneasy feeling didn't go away, nor did it grow stronger, as it had in some past circumstances.

When I arrived home, I explained to Vicki what had happened and about the uneasiness I was feeling. We agreed to sit on it until the contract came and then decide. A few weeks later the contract arrived. At this point the more I thought and prayed, the more uneasy I felt. Louise, who was now moving in her own prophetic gift, confirmed my uneasiness with her response to my email, saying, "I'm not feeling warm and fuzzy about this." I printed the contract and let the rest of the family know we'd received it.

"No!" replied our oldest, twenty-two-year-old Sara, without hesitation.

"I live in California, so it doesn't affect me," replied Daniel, who was twenty-one at the time and stayed in California after attending ministry school there.

"I don't think this is really good for our family," Vicki said. I agreed but wanted to talk to everyone and make it a family decision since it would possibly change all our lives. We all sat at the kitchen table and discussed the possibility.

"I don't want it," Paul, our eleven-year-old, chimed in.

"Whatever you guys think," said Krissy, who was fourteen.

Our nine-year-old, Michael, had an unusual look on his face. "What's wrong?" I asked him.

"Dad, does this mean the camera people will follow me to school?"

"Probably," I replied.

"Then I don't want it. What would my friends think? I wouldn't like that," Michael said.

Since we were all in agreement, the decision was clear. The more I prayed about it, the more uneasy I got, but I took my time responding because I really wanted to be sure one way or the other. I sent the producer an email a few weeks later to set up a call to discuss the offer. "I'm honored to be given the opportunity," I told them, "but we are declining the offer. Maybe sometime in the future." I thanked them for their time and thought that would be the end of our relationship, but it wasn't. Since that exchange I have spoken to them on several occasions and even prophesied over them. It became clear that the uneasiness I was feeling was direction from the Holy Spirit to decline the reality show offer. But He gave me the go-ahead to meet the producer and her husband because He had a bigger purpose for me—to deliver prophetic words to them.

Through situations like this I have learned some lessons. When you don't sense a clear, definitive yes or no from the Holy Spirit, or if you have an uneasiness-but-proceed signal, allow the situation to develop. But keep praying and remain sensitive to the Holy Spirit with your eyes and ears open. Also, keep your guard up. Discernment and answers will come in time as God reveals them. After that, seek counsel and prayer from trustworthy, like-minded believers. If the matter involves others, get their input to see if you reach one accord. Always be open to either a yes or a no in a situation. In the previous example, I discerned, "Proceed with caution," and the Holy Spirit eventually revealed His plan—no to the TV show but yes to meeting the producers so prophecies could be delivered.

Aligned for His Purpose

As God divinely positioned my meetings with SQuire and Louise, we were brought into further alignment as our relationship grew. That connection paved the way for me to eventually meet Kathie Lee Gifford, which set another prophetic sequence into motion—I'll share that later in the book. Kathie Lee is a good friend of theirs, and the Lord had a prophetic message for her. Again, I didn't push. Things simply unfolded as I stayed sensitive and obedient to God's leading.

Our obedience is critical to the moving forward of God's plans. If I had not given the word on the phone to SQuire and Louise, God certainly could have found someone else to deliver the message they needed to hear. He will do that. Yet at other times if we disobey, God's work goes undone, and there are consequences. Though I fall short, I strive to listen and obey, and He has been faithful to use me as He sees fit. If God can trust you with His gift, then there really isn't a limit on what He can do in you and through you.

I've seen it happen again and again—one act of obedience can change the courses of lives and ministries. One phone call introduced SQuire and Louise to the spiritual gift of prophecy and set me up to give them prophetic counsel concerning their own ministry and Godwinks business. Louise and other believers around them began to further their prophetic gifts. They had been praying for revival, and Vicki and I have prayed with them, encouraged them, comforted them, and ministered to them to help them develop and steward their prophetic gifts.

Equally, SQuire and Louise have poured their love and wisdom into our lives. They've become personal friends and role models to Vicki and me, showing us how to have a godly marriage, honor God in business, and handle ourselves in public ministry. Although SQuire and Louise were initially strangers to me, I quickly felt at ease with them and, as I mentioned earlier, was impressed with how they interacted with each other. Their compatibility was evident, and I was struck by the respect they showed for each other and how clear it was that their marriage was an equal partnership. At one point, they disagreed over a particular detail of a story they were telling me, but Louise handled it with humor and grace. This made me smile and gave me comfort. They have been an example of a marriage and ministry partnership as God intended.

Our meeting had been divinely arranged, just as every God assignment is, and through it the Lord's purposes were fulfilled. We never have to make things happen. As I will discuss in later chapters, all we have to do is step out in obedience. God will do the rest.

Moving in the prophetic flow can affect and strengthen every aspect of our lives. It is all about allowing God to position us for His opportunities so He can bring us and those around us into alignment to fulfill our divine destinies.

Chapter 2

Facing Our Issues

WHEN OPERATING IN the prophetic, brace yourself for change. Quite often the word you give to someone else is pointing back to you. As you begin to move forward in administering the gifts God has given to you, particularly the prophetic gift, don't be surprised if you are challenged to grow in your walk with God at a quick pace. You may even be more challenged to grow than the ones to whom you are ministering.

God's goal is to bring all His children into unity with Him and into conformity to the image of Jesus. The apostle Paul wrote, "For those whom He foreknew, He predestined to be conformed to the image of His Son" (Rom. 8:29, MEV). Everything God is doing in and through us, including through our gifts to others, is to ultimately make us more like Jesus. Therefore, when God changes your life and moves you forward in your ministry calling, you will encounter issues that God wants you to deal with.

One time the Holy Spirit had me prophesy to a woman concerning some issues from her past. After I ministered to her, she questioned what was said and was visibly upset. She felt that what I shared was not relevant, as she believed the issues from her past had been resolved. Instead of seeking God to see if there were, in fact, some unresolved issues from her past, she took her anger out on me and provided some negative "feedback." This, in turn, exposed issues of my own that I thought were behind me but that clearly still needed to be dealt with.

My point is, if you desire to walk in an authentic prophetic ministry, you must also desire to grow deeper in your spiritual walk. That means being willing to confront the issues in your life that the Holy Spirit shines His light on. Putting God first means dying to self, dealing with those past issues, and being willing to change your priorities.

Looking back on my own life and prophetic ministry, I've seen how the Lord has brought past issues to the surface every so often to teach me. I experienced a lot of rejection and racism when I was younger. My way of dealing with those issues was to assume people always wanted something from me or wanted to use me. To protect myself, I always kept my guard up and tried to anticipate what people wanted. Then I would regulate my reactions to protect myself from being taken advantage of. As I became more well known for the prophetic, I found myself doing a lot of calculating, but I was still getting taken advantage of more and more.

People would say things such as, "Oh, I traveled all this way because God told me that you have a prophetic word for me." There would be no prophetic word because the Holy Spirit didn't give me anything, so this terrible feeling of failure would come over me. One time I was at a New Year's Eve party, sitting on the couch and hanging out with some friends. A guy whom I had just met came into the living room, sat across from me, and started looking at me. He continued to stare at me for three hours. Yes, three hours! I fell asleep on the couch, and when I woke up, he was still staring at me, waiting for a prophetic word. Do you know how uncomfortable that makes a person? Yet he didn't care. He was determined to get a prophetic word.

I was at another party, a birthday party, when the guests started asking me if I had a prophetic word for the birthday person. They placed the microphone in my hands as if I had the power to turn on the prophetic gift. Prophecy is a sovereign gift of God, and some people want to manipulate it. As they put the microphone in my hands, I rolled my eyes. Yes, I was frustrated.

Some people follow me around wherever I go, looking for a word. This really turns me off. A lot of times they will keep following me and then ask, "You got something for me?"

I say, "No, I don't have anything."

"You sure?"

"Yes, I'm sure."

"Can you ask God?"

"Um, yes, I did already."

Another time, I was invited to appear as a guest on a Christian television show. I flew in, went to my room to drop off my luggage, and went downstairs to the studio to watch the current day's taping. I sat in the back of the studio audience, listening to the guests, minding my own business. I didn't think to call security because I was in the last row. I didn't realize it, but people started congregating behind me and formed what became a long line. Security came and got upset with me because a line like that in the studio audience could be distracting to the guests being interviewed. I apologized for the possible interruption and went back to my room. I just wanted to be like everybody else, but unfortunately I wasn't able to.

Most people probably mean well, but nobody wants to be taken advantage of like that. It makes you feel used, like people don't care about you as a person and are interested in you only because they want a prophetic word. Then, when you don't have something for them, most just disappear. I have come to realize that the people seeking a prophetic word from me may think they won't have an opportunity like that again, so I have more grace about it now. God has given each of us a responsibility to steward the gift He has given us, and being manipulated into using the gift creates undue pressure. There's a lot more to operating in the prophetic than just giving someone a prophetic word and moving on. Keeping yourself available to be used by God requires sacrifice. It takes a physical and mental toll, and you open yourself up to being taken advantage of by people.

Now, if the Holy Spirit is directing a person to me, that's one thing. He does do that from time to time, but He will let me know. I emphasize *He* will let me know. That's why I try to stay pliable and listen for His voice. Yet when people use their circumstances to manipulate me into coming up with a word for them, that's when my walls go up. When God wants to speak a prophetic word to a stranger, it's because He loves them. I don't know the stranger or have any feelings toward them, but I still have to go through the sacrifice and experience the effects of it because God loves them so much. Sometimes even when a person is manipulating the situation, God does want you to speak to them. You have to follow what He wants you to do. If I've walked away from someone who seemed to be seeking a prophetic word, I usually go back to them and say, "Hey, I have something to tell you."

Here is a case in point: At the birthday party after they put the microphone in my hands and I rolled my eyes, they kept asking, and I definitely felt manipulated, but then to my surprise the Holy Spirit showed up! I got the nudge and stood up to speak. The words started to flow, and the Holy Spirit was faithful to speak to the person, but when it was over, I sat down, feeling resentful. I thought, "I can't do anything or go anywhere without this thing going off." I was referring to God's gift as "this thing." This shows how frustrated I had become.

As I sat down, Vicki leaned over to me and told me sternly, "Honey, you have to be careful of your attitude. Don't roll your eyes." I felt angry and was going to say something stern back to her when she said, "You rolled your eyes, and it was recorded on the video." Just as she said it, I felt so ashamed. The Lord gave me a special gift, and here I was complaining about it. I personally witnessed it bringing joy, encouragement, restoration, and hope to people, and all I could think about was how I felt. It was a real low point in my walk, and I could no longer ignore the fact that I had some serious issues going on inside me. I wish I could say the revelation changed my attitude overnight, but sadly it did not. Even though I was aware of the situation, I had not gotten that way overnight, and freedom would not come overnight. But I immediately stopped rolling my eyes. I never did it again, but my heart did not fully change. I still felt the frustration of being used and manipulated.

The prophetic gift required so much emotional energy that it became exhausting and eventually started pulling me down. I had always been under the impression we should serve the Lord wholeheartedly and be happy about it, but just the opposite was happening. I was losing myself and becoming frustrated with the gift taking over my life. Instead of experiencing more joy, I grew more tiresome. Not only were people using me, but it seemed as if everywhere I went, I would feel the nudge to speak to someone—on vacation, out to eat, at the grocery store. I was like, "Oh,

I have to serve. I have to serve. I have to serve." And in all my serving, my life got lost.

It got to the point where some days I didn't even want to speak to people, but the nudging would continue, so I did it. I wasn't happy about it, but I wanted to be obedient to the Lord. I remember being on vacation one time and really needing a break, but almost every day, I was prompted to speak to someone. Just as I would start to get upset, however, I would realize that I really didn't want to take a vacation from God or for Him to take a vacation from covering my family and me. Still, the more I pressed forward, the more frustrated I became and the more the Lord needed to deal with those serious issues inside me.

Sudden Recognition

My first glimpse of how the prophetic gift would affect my life happened soon after David Tyree made his now-famous helmet catch during the 2008 national football championship. I had prophesied that God was going to bring him out of obscurity into the spotlight and give him a platform and he would be known as a wide receiver rather than simply a special-teams player, and those things came to pass as a result of his game-changing catch. So when "the catch" garnered worldwide recognition, my name got attached to it, and I received worldwide recognition too. This was a completely new and totally unexpected experience for me.

Along with this sudden notoriety came more people looking for me. Vicki and I were invited to dinners, birthday parties, church events, you name it, just because people now wanted to hang out with us. The problem was, we barely knew these people. But after a while I grew weary of resisting and just started to go with the flow of what was happening. Life started to change, and when it did, it felt like a tidal wave that I could not hold back. Though these prophetic words spoken from my mouth were confirmed and amazingly supernatural, I was scared that the tidal wave was pulling me under and I would drown. Instead of all the attention I just wanted to be left alone and feel safe.

When the gift inside me didn't let up, I became depressed and conflicted. It felt as if there was a competition under way for my priorities: God versus my job and family. Initially I would cry out to the Lord, "Please let me have a regular day and let the prophetic gift calm down." But it didn't. In fact, the nudges increased. It was during this time that many of those issues buried in my heart started to surface. I could not run from or suppress them any longer.

Because of all the rejection I had experienced growing up, I was driven to succeed. My self-worth was tied up with my work. Staying focused on my work and achieving success in the business world were a way to suppress the hurt and distract me from the pain I felt. Then, when the prophetic gift was activated, my drive to succeed shifted to it, and I began to evaluate myself based on my performance when operating in the prophetic. The feelings of rejection were amplified if people wanted the gift but not me, and my self-worth was reduced to zero if I didn't perform well. I felt I had lost myself. I didn't know who I was due to people's expectations of me, and I knew I could not possibly meet those expectations.

Your *identity* is who you feel you are. Your *self-worth* is how much you feel you matter. The feeling of being used and taken advantage of intensified, causing my rejection and identity issues to fester inside me. I felt like a walking time bomb about to explode. The Lord had to get me to deal with these issues, or I was going to be consumed by them and hurt myself and the ones I loved most.

One day I was speaking to a friend and mentioned my frustration. He looked at me, smiled, and said, "You know, Hubie, you have to deal with your rejection issues, Brother! These people don't want you; they want to use your gift, and you need to come to terms with it." All through the night and the next day my friend's words replayed through my mind. It was like a song stuck in an endless loop. I had lost my identity and was having trouble finding it. I didn't know who I really was anymore. I wasn't a prophet. I was Hubie.

I spent the next couple of days thinking about who I really was and came to terms with myself. I am Hubie, a child of God, nothing more and nothing less. I am a certified public accountant by trade, which is a gift. I am a prophetic minister, and this also is a gift. So now I could distinguish between my gifts and my identity and reconcile and departmentalize those things. This was a profound revelation that changed the way I looked at life. I saw that it was possible to serve in different roles when needed and still be myself.

I can relax and just be Hubie. I am not this high, holy person or whatever some people see me as. I certainly don't see myself as anything like that. I am just struggling through life like everybody else. We just all have different gifts and callings, that's all. I'm a simple guy. What I write is simple. The way I talk is simple. The way I minister is simple. I've met people who use all these huge words. They know church history like the back of their hand. And they know Scripture far better than I do, but do you know what? It's OK. That doesn't bother me any longer. We're all wired different ways, and I'm comfortable with that. I don't think I'm better than anybody else. When people look at me and are like, "Oh, the man of God is here," I just reach out my hand and say, "What's your name? Let's chat and hang out."

This revelation about my identity and value enabled me to move forward with a fresh view. In fact, looking back, I can see that the David Tyree prophecy was a test to prepare me for what was to come.

After I later prophesied to Jonathan Cahn in the airport about the book he had just written, *The Harbinger*, it became a worldwide phenomenon and a *New York Times* best seller. In turn, my visibility shot up to an even higher level! But because of the lessons I had learned, I was able to handle the notoriety much better than before.

The bottom line is, I've learned that the prophetic gift

is God's, not mine. God allows me to use it when He wants me to, and that understanding relieves a lot of pressure. This prophetic gift is like a tool that I put away in a toolbox when I am done. It stays there until the Lord takes it out and puts it in my hand. Then I use it.

Lean In to What God Wants to Do in Your Life

As I have allowed the Lord to deal with the issues that have surfaced in my life, I have learned several keys that help me surrender to Him and walk confidently in the gift He has given me. These principles are true for all of us, regardless of what ministry gift we've been given.

Put God first.

In our lives there's a spiritual battle between the spirit and the flesh. It's a battle to determine whom we're going to serve. The same is true when it comes to walking in the prophetic. To be used to our full potential as vessels to declare the Holy Spirit's words, we have to learn to die to self. However, dying to self does not mean dying to who you are and how God created you. There is a difference. The key is to be pliable and put His will over our own. When we do, everything else will fall into place. In the Book of Psalms, David says, "I delight to do Your will, O my God, and Your law is within my heart" (Ps. 40:8). And Jesus said to His disciples, "If anyone will come after Me, let him deny himself, and take up his cross, and follow Me.

For whoever would save his life will lose it, and whoever loses his life for My sake will find it" (Matt. 16:24–25, MEV).

Putting God first means dealing with your past issues when the Holy Spirit shines His light on them and being willing to change your priorities and the way you're used to living. It's about trusting that the Lord wants what is best for us, that He desires our ultimate healing and freedom. Remember, as born-again children of God, we walk in newness of life.

> Therefore we were buried with Him by baptism into death, that just as Christ was raised up from the dead by the glory of the Father, even so we also should walk in newness of life.
>
> —ROMANS 6:4, MEV

> Therefore, if anyone is in Christ, he is a new creation; old things have passed away; behold, all things have become new.
>
> —2 CORINTHIANS 5:17

Don't isolate yourself.

Stay in community. Allow spiritual fathers, mothers, and mentors to pour into your life. You can become arrogant if you are isolated. Instead, we need to be in fellowship with other believers. The Bible says, "And let us consider one another to provoke unto love and to good works" (Heb. 10:24, KJV).

The apostle Paul wrote concerning one of his friends in the faith, "For I long to see you, that I may impart to you some spiritual gift, so that you may be established—that is, that I may be encouraged together with you by the mutual faith both of you and me" (Rom. 1:11–12). All of us have gifts that others need. Paul wanted to impart his gift and receive his friend's gifts. Growing in the fullness that God has for us requires giving our gifts and receiving the gifts of others.

Stay true to who you are.

Learn to be comfortable in your own skin. Just be yourself, and don't try to be someone else. Do the work God gave you to do, not someone else's. Don't compare yourself either, or you will feel pressured to live up to others' expectations and become vulnerable to being manipulated. "For we are His workmanship, created in Christ Jesus for good works, which God prepared beforehand, so that we should walk in them" (Eph. 2:10, MEV). God created you for *your* purpose for *His* glory. Staying true to yourself takes faith and trust that God knows best.

Your gift is not your identity or a measure of your self-worth.

If you base your value on how well you prophesy, you will experience issues with rejection and failure. For example, if you go out to prophesy and have a bad night, you're going to feel horrible if you place your value in your performance, because you'll feel you're worth nothing. This is true whether your gift is prophecy or singing or playing ball. Your identity and self-worth cannot be in your performance but in who you are. If you received Jesus, your identity is in Him regardless of what you do or how you perform. "Yet to all who did receive him, to those who believed in his name, he gave the right to become children of God" (John 1:12, NIV). If you are in Christ, you are a child of God. Separate your identity as a child of God from your role as a minister when you're using your spiritual gift.

God is in control of all things, including your future.

God goes *before* us, walks alongside us, and has our backs. "And the Lord, He is the One who goes before you. He will be with you, He will not leave you nor forsake you; do not fear nor be dismayed" (Deut. 31:8). God knows what He can do through you. He created you and knows you completely, so let Him take the lead. David prayed, "O Lord, You have searched me and known me. You know my sitting down and my rising up; You understand my thought afar off. You comprehend my path and my lying down, and are acquainted with all my ways" (Ps. 139:1–3). It takes a lot of trust in the Lord to obey Him when you don't want to or when you don't believe you can do it, especially when moving forward in the prophetic. But you can trust that He knows all things, and He knows you better than you know yourself.

God has His reasons for choosing to work through you.

Often God chooses the weak things to confound the wise (1 Cor. 1:27). "'For My thoughts are not your thoughts, nor are your ways My ways,' says the LORD. 'For as the heavens are higher than the earth, so are My ways higher than your ways, and My thoughts than your thoughts'" (Isa. 55:8–9). Understanding that God is in control changes the way you minister to people and the way you connect to new relationships. It even changes you.

God works in stages to reveal your issues so you're able to resolve them a bit at a time, like peeling back layers of an onion. God knows more about you and what He can do through you than you do. So you have to die to yourself, which means you must die to your need to control. Trust Him and let Him lead, even if you don't particularly know the purposes of what He's doing in you.

Remember, the Lord is just as interested in dealing with your issues as He is in dealing with those you are ministering to. The purpose of every gift from God is ultimately to assist all of us in becoming more like Jesus and experiencing healing and freedom. So relax, be yourself, and let the gift inside you blossom.

Chapter 3

It's OK to Be Yourself

To be all that God wants us to be, we have to let go and put our full faith in Him. It is one thing to say that; it's quite another to actually walk it out. Due to our insecurities and fears, we are reluctant to turn everything over to Him with complete trust. In several areas of my own life I had to come to the point where I believed the Lord knew more than I did and that He had my best interest in mind. Only then could I finally let go and let Him lead, knowing He would get me where I needed to go safely. One of those areas involved trusting God with how He created me and learning to rest in being myself instead of trying to be like somebody else. It sounds simple, but actually doing it was anything but.

People called me "prophet," "man of God," "God's mouthpiece," and other monumental titles. Being perceived and accepted as such made me feel incredibly uneasy because I knew how unworthy and unqualified I was, and still am, to wear those labels. People elevated me as a symbol, which heightened the insecurity that stemmed from my growing up in a lower-income part of town. What's more, I held prophets in the Bible in such high regard that I could not picture myself the same way. Under the immense pressure of trying to live up to people's expectations, I went to God, and He told me to be myself and do what I do, to trust Him despite my feelings of inadequacy. But like I said, walking this out is not that easy. It's only a matter of time before the Lord stretches your faith by putting you in situations that challenge those feelings of inadequacy.

The more I was exposed to the prophetic, the more I saw how radically different I was from others in prophetic ministry. This made me even more insecure. "Is something wrong with me?" I wondered more times than I care to count. "Why am I so different? Am I using the gift the right way? Is it truly from God? Is it witchcraft? Is what I'm doing really led by the Holy Spirit?" On and on the questions went, and I truly did not know the answers. I was scared of doing anything unbiblical, but in those early days I had no idea what I was doing, so I learned to intercede all through the day.

I had no formal training in the prophetic and never attended a ministry school or received a Bible college degree or any kind of certification. I had never been formally commissioned or recognized as a prophet in any type of public setting or church service and didn't know how to act in front of an audience. All I knew was this gift was inside me, and when I felt the nudge, the word had to come out. It was bigger than me, and I really couldn't control it.

The gift started flowing one day as I prayed for a woman in Sweden while on a missionary trip. I thought I was simply praying, and a prophetic word just began rising up from inside me and poured out. After that I continued to move forward despite having unanswered questions, because the fruit was obviously from God. I couldn't deny that some of what I was witnessing was truly miraculous.

I don't want to give you the impression that I'm a lone ranger with no spiritual covering or accountability. I've always tried to submit myself to a pastor and other biblically solid leadership, but they didn't have all the answers I needed. However, God always provides the things necessary to equip those He has called. He has been faithful to bring mentors into my life at strategic points in time to answer some of my questions and help me along. Not all my questions were fully answered, but when God calls us to something, there will always remain some element of stepping into the unknown, which keeps us in a posture of trusting Him.

My friend Jack Forde was my first mentor and role model. He exemplified godly character and discipline. One of the major things he taught me was to look above my circumstances. Basically he taught me to not get lost or paralyzed staring at things in front of me but to do my best to look above the circumstances to see what is really going on. Think of it as getting a bird's-eye view of the situation. There is always more going on than meets the eye, both in the spiritual and physical realms, and we need to be aware. I don't know what I would have done if Jack had not come into my life when he did. He was able to mentor me by his actions first and then his words. Jack was a prayer warrior, and he knew how to pray. He actually enjoyed praying all night. Watching his prayer life showed me what could be done, so I didn't really have an excuse for not seeking God.

After I grasped what Jack taught me and began applying those principles, the Lord brought Joseph Mattera into my life. He moved in the office of prophet at one time and is now a bishop. Joseph needed an accountant, and while working on his account, I sensed the Holy Spirit nudging me with a word for him. Joseph recognized the prophetic call on my life, and he became a prophetic mentor who would answer many of my nagging questions since he had a lot more experience than I did. These two men have had such a great impact on my life, but it is important to note that I never stopped what I was doing even though I had questions without answers. My relationship with God was strong enough to keep me moving forward in the midst of many unknowns. Little did I realize God was using His times of silence to build my faith. Though alone and unsure, I knew that when the Lord directed me to open my mouth, He would fill it.

An Unofficial Commissioning

One day I was with my friend Papa San, who is a Jamaican reggae and gospel singer. I was staying at his house in Florida with him and his wife, Debbie. Papa San came up to me and said, "Hey, we're going to see Auntie Cherry, aka Winsome Williams, tonight. Is that OK?" I didn't know anything about this Auntie Cherry, but since he had invited me to stay at his home, I said, "OK."

We arrived at her house, and as soon as we walked through the front door, we were overtaken by the amazing aroma of Jamaican home cooking. I love Jamaican food, so this was definitely a place I wanted to be! I closed my eyes and for a moment just inhaled the smells and warmth surrounding me. Auntie Cherry greeted us, and before we knew it, she had served us a plate. Then the room got quiet as everyone started eating. The fact that everyone was concentrating on eating tells you how good it was.

While I was enjoying the meal, Auntie Cherry started asking me questions about myself and how I knew Papa San. Then, out of the blue, she asked, "Were you a missionary?" I thought it was a strange question but replied, "Yes, I have been on many missionary trips. How did you know?"

She laughed and said, "You ate everything on the plate, including the spices, which people don't usually eat!"

"If you give me more food, I will eat more spices!" I replied.

We all had a good laugh, but there was something unusually special about her. When she laughed, it filled the house with the presence of joy. After we ate, Auntie Cherry scooted her chair up next to me, and the two of us began to do some serious talking. As we did, a strange thing happened. When she started asking questions about me, my face moved close to hers even though she could hear me clearly. I mean, my face was right up into her face. Something came over me, and I couldn't stop. I must have looked like a crazy person with my face so close to hers, and she looked annoyed, but for some reason I kept doing it. Something was compelling me to do it. Was it the Holy Spirit? I wasn't really sure what it was.

Maybe a half hour passed, and she suggested we go upstairs to talk. I told Papa San I was going upstairs with Auntie Cherry and followed her upstairs. Feeling cautious, this time I kept my distance. While on the road I learned a rule to always try to keep my distance with everyone, which I had just totally broken when staring Auntie Cherry in the face. She went into her bedroom, and I cautiously hesitated at the door. "It's OK," she said, waving at me to come in. "The door will stay open." I figured with the door open and Papa San downstairs it was safe, so I proceeded into the bedroom.

Auntie Cherry sat down on the foot of the bed and then stared at me as if she were looking through me. It was something I hadn't experienced before. The whole encounter was strange. As she was glaring at me, she asked, "You got something to tell me?" I was about ready to reply with "What do you mean?" when words started flowing from my mouth. They continued to flow for a while, and tears filled her eyes. Whatever was coming out was really getting to her, because she started to weep. I got her a tissue from the top of the dresser, and she wiped away her tears.

After she gathered herself, we spoke a little while longer about her journey and how she got stuck. We talked about how she had been hurt and how hard it was for her to move forward from the experience. I told her I understood because I had worked through similar issues. God was letting her know that He was with her, she did not have to fear, and everything was going to be OK, so she could move forward with her gift. Now that she was free, she could start again.

As it turned out Auntie Cherry was a prophetess, and some tough things happened to her at church that caused her to get stuck. For a while she didn't want to prophesy anymore, but now she felt God calling her to move forward with her gift again. The problem was, she didn't know how to start over. As she received the prophetic word from the Holy Spirit, you could see the joy return to her. I encouraged her that she still had the gift and to go forward, taking baby steps until she built her confidence back.

Then, all of a sudden, Auntie Cherry's eyes locked onto mine with an intensity I hadn't seen in her before, and she became very serious. She got up from the bed and moved her face close to mine, just as I had done to her earlier.

Looking me dead in the eye, she said in her most stern, authoritarian voice, "Sit down on the bed!"

"Yes, ma'am," I said. The way she was talking to me, I had only two choices: comply or run! I chose to sit. She reached for a bottle of olive oil on the dresser, opened it, and said, "I have to anoint your loins."

"Um…OK," I said.

She anointed me and poured oil over my head. My eyes were closed, and I could feel the oil dripping off my hair, down the side of my face, and onto my neck. Then, again, with great authority she said, "Hubie!"

My eyes popped open, and I replied, "Yes?"

She said, "It is OK for you to not recognize yourself for what you are, but you cannot do that to other people! They see you as something, and you cannot reject it anymore because it is who you truly are." She glared at me and continued, "Do you know what that means?"

"Um, yes," I said. "I know what that means."

Up to that point people were calling me a prophet of God, and I did not know how to handle it, so I'd just say, "Nah, not me." Sometimes trying to be funny, I'd joke, "I can't be a prophet because my last name is Synn," or, "I am an accountant, and I deal with profit and loss." To this day I have never had a prophetic word from anyone spoken over me with so much authority that it physically shook me. I guess you could say her anointing me was my official commissioning into the ministry office of the prophet.

After that Auntie Cherry ministered to me about some

other prophetic questions I had at the time. She became another mentor of mine, imparting much-needed insight to me during that season in my life. She came to visit us in New Jersey one time, and she gave Vicki and me a prophetic word. Noticing our relationship with our son Daniel was strained, she prophesied, "The Lord is going to heal that relationship, and it will be very strong." Sensing it was from God, we clung to that prophetic word during the difficult times, and it gave us hope. There were times I thought the word she gave would not come to pass, but though it took years, in the end she was correct and our relationship was healed.

As time went on, I had more questions—and more frustration when the answers didn't come as fast as I wanted. Thankfully the Lord is more patient than I am. Invariably it seemed that just as I would be on the verge of giving up and feeling as if He'd taken a vacation, the Lord would send someone across my path to bring me the answers I sought. Once, I was invited to be a guest on the *Marcus & Joni* show on Daystar Television. Before the taping, I was sitting in the greenroom waiting to go on when a man entered the room. He was tall and skinny and had a gray beard. At first glance he kind of looked like Kenny Rogers. He walked up to me, shook my hand, and said, "Hello."

"Hi," I replied. "My name is Hubie."

"My name is John Paul," he said with a kind smile. "I'm a friend of Marcus and Joni."

When he looked at me, the anointing and love of God

radiated from him. The best way I can describe it is to say his presence lit up the room. We sat down at the table with some food, and as we were eating and chatting, I started to get the familiar nudge, and then my stomach started churning. He noticed I wasn't eating and asked if I was OK. I replied that I was nervous about being on the show since it was a new experience for me. He smiled and said, "Don't worry. It will be OK. Marcus and Joni are great people." Then my stomach felt worse, and I said, "John Paul? The Lord wants to tell you something."

He smiled and said, "OK."

As the words were coming out of my mouth, he was absorbing them and concentrating on what was being said. The prophecy was a long one, and afterward John Paul gave his warm smile and relaxed. "Hubie," he said, "that was something. Thank you. I haven't received a word like that in about ten years." He paused for a moment to reflect before continuing. "You know, I have a prophetic ministry."

"You do?" I said. "I didn't know."

As we chatted, John Paul asked about my gift, and I asked him about his. "I see newspaper headlines," he said. "You?"

I told him how my gift worked, and he nodded his head. He seemed to understand me, but before we could talk about my gift, we were called to go on the show. During the taping John Paul started to discuss the gift I have. He opened his Bible and said, "It's like when the Spirit of the Lord came over Mary and as the Spirit of the Lord came over David. That is what you have, Hubie."

Not knowing how to react to such an affirmation, I sat there feeling humbled and honored, almost a little embarrassed. But the more I thought about it, the more I dismissed what he said about the way my gift flowed, thinking, "No way!"

After the show we exchanged information to keep in touch. While I was flying home later that night, I kept thinking about what John Paul said. I googled him and was amazed at what I found. I saw that John Paul Jackson was well seasoned in the prophetic. I now had someone else in my life who could help me understand my gift. I communicated with him over the following couple of months just to say hello and that I was praying for him.

John Paul described the category of prophetic expression, or type, that I moved in as an "ecstatic prophet." This basically means that the Spirit of God comes over a person.

John Paul and I experienced such a special time of connection. Unfortunately, John Paul got sick and passed away. Though I knew he was in heaven with the Lord, I was very upset over it. And there were so many questions I wanted to ask him, but it never felt like the right time. He was a great man of God, and I will always treasure the time and conversations we had in that short period.

After John Paul passed, I wasn't sure what to do about my unanswered questions, so I did nothing. I simply went back to my regular routine. I thought about what John Paul told me about the Spirit of God coming over me like David and Mary and reasoned that it really couldn't be true. Despite all the confirmations from my mentors Jack, Joseph, Auntie Cherry, and now John Paul Jackson, I still saw myself as undeserving, so I just blew off their words and stopped thinking about them.

I met Jonathan Cahn, author of *The Harbinger*, at the airport, and it was an incredible divine appointment. I talk about it in my first book, *The Tales of a Wandering Prophet*. After that meeting Vicki and I would occasionally visit Jonathan's congregation. We loved the services, and Vicki and I were learning a lot about the Old Testament. One day when we were attending Jonathan's congregation, he had a special guest speaker named Rogerio, who was a prophet from South America. Rogerio did not even speak English, so he had a translator.

After Rogerio spoke, he started to walk around the crowd and minister to individuals. It was a crowd of several hundred, and we were in the middle of the last section. The next thing I knew, Rogerio looked directly at me. When our eyes met, he walked toward me. I looked away, and when I looked back, I could see he was headed directly toward me. He came and stood in front of me, asked me to stand up, and then started to prophesy to me. He said, "You are this small, shy man, but when the Spirit of the Lord comes over you, then you open your mouth like a lion roaring." There was more to the prophecy, but that opening line really hit me hard. He basically said the same thing John Paul had said earlier about the Spirit of the Lord coming over me.

Over the next few days, I thought a lot about what John

Paul and Rogerio had told me. It finally brought me comfort and peace because I knew I was going in the right direction. I still had unanswered questions, but at least I had peace about where I was at that point, and that was enough. Every now and then more questions would pop up and I wasn't sure how to answer them, but I had learned to be patient, keep moving forward, and wait on the Lord.

A Lingering Question

One of my nagging questions that had not been answered was why I get sick when the Lord wants me to prophesy. Why did the Lord choose that sign as a way of confirming what He wants me to do? Whenever I would talk about this sign with other prophetic ministers who saw things in the spirit realm, they would shrug their shoulders and say things such as, "That doesn't happen to me," or, "That is different," or, "Better you than me." I began to notice a pattern, that the Lord saw fit to answer my questions one at a time, over a period of time, through people He sent into my life. Now I wanted to know more about this sign and wasn't sure where to look. Again, little did I realize, the Lord was setting me up to meet the person who would answer this lingering question.

While attending the annual International Coalition of Apostolic Leaders (ICAL) conference in Dallas, I was waiting in a lunch line when the Lord nudged me to focus on a couple who were in line ahead of me. I kept watching them as the line moved forward, and I eventually followed them to their table. There was an empty seat, so I sat down and introduced myself. John McElroy introduced himself and his wife, Alaine, telling me they were from Australia. The moment I introduced myself, my stomach started to hurt. I hadn't eaten yet, so I knew what it meant.

Rather than stalling, as I usually do, I just let the word pour forth because I felt something different about this couple. We had made small talk for a while, and when I sensed the Holy Spirit saying it was time, I told them I had a prophetic word for them and began to share it. I spoke first to John and then Alaine. They smiled afterward and asked, "Have you ever thought about going to Australia?"

"Not really," I said, "but I'm open to what the Lord wants."

"Maybe one day you and your wife could visit and stay with us," they replied.

"Maybe one day," I replied. "Thank you for the offer."

I smiled because we have invited so many people to stay at our house. It was heartwarming to know someone else was doing the same thing. I didn't think much more about it since Australia is halfway across the world. I just ate my lunch and went back to the conference. About six months later, John texted me that he had some friends visiting New York City and he wanted me to meet with them. I had a packed schedule with accounting work, but I managed to rearrange a day to meet with them. Accounting deadlines often cause a lot of stress, but when I feel the Lord wants me to meet someone, I try to make the time and put His agenda first.

I met Mark and Belinda Godfrey in New York City for lunch. I wasn't exactly sure why they wanted to meet, but I was certain something was up. After lunch we went for coffee, and the Lord had something to say to Belinda first and then Mark. They were great people, and I was thankful to spend time with them for a few hours. It was a divine appointment, as it felt as if I had known them for years even though we had just met. They thanked me for taking time out of my busy schedule to meet with them and asked if we could stay in contact. I said sure, and we traded texts from time to time just to check on each other.

One day they asked if I would be interested in going to Australia. They were sponsoring a conference in Perth, Australia, called the Beyond Prophetic Summit. I told them I would pray about it and let them know. I have learned from numerous people to always pause and seek God before I give an answer about a speaking engagement. I had always wanted to visit Australia because I wanted to see a real kangaroo, but it was halfway around the world, and I knew traveling there would take a toll. I'd be away from home for at least a week, maybe two. The jet lag was going to be rough, not to mention prophetic ministry is always physically draining.

The more I thought about it, the less appealing it became. Yet the more I prayed about it, the more the Lord kept telling me I needed to go. I resisted for a few days, until I started to lose sleep over it. Finally, I gave in and texted Mark to say we should talk about it. I Skyped with Mark and Belinda shortly afterward and agreed to take the trip to minister in Perth, Australia. A few months later I was on my way to the conference and had no clue that God would use the experience to expose my feelings of insecurity and inadequacy, bring healing to me, and answer some lingering questions.

I landed in Australia at about ten o'clock in the evening, and Mark picked me up at the airport. I was staying with them, which was great. All of us, including their children, really bonded. It helped me since I was missing my family from the moment I boarded the plane and headed to Perth. All I could think about on the flight was how much I already missed them. I slept well the first night at the Godfreys due to the long flight and was ready to go the next morning.

My first meeting was at John McElroy's church, which seemed surreal, since the last time I saw him was in Dallas. I walked in and saw John. He greeted me with a warm smile and said, "I can't believe you are here."

"Me neither!" I responded.

We gave each other hugs, and he introduced me to everyone. John had gathered his leaders in the room, so after the introductions he allowed me to start ministering to them. After we were done, we had lunch before the next scheduled meeting that afternoon for Christian leaders in the area. Mark and Belinda's ministry was sponsoring it. Often when someone is visiting internationally, the event hosts prefer to maximize time with guest speakers, so appointments with church leaders and congregants throughout Perth had been scheduled to take place before the actual conference started. I'm not moved by crowds—it's about people over the platform, so I was eager to meet everyone.

A man walked into the back room and introduced himself to me as one of the conference speakers. He shook my hand and said his name was David Balestri. When the meeting was ready to begin, I looked over at David, and I could tell the anointing of God was all over him. He seemed extremely knowledgeable and was a fashionable dresser. I have to admit, I was pretty intimidated while sitting next to him on the stage and wasn't sure what to expect.

The meeting began, and the host asked both of us questions. David gave great, detailed answers while I stumbled over my responses. Being nervous didn't help the situation. I kept wondering, "Why am I here?" When it came time to minister, David prayed in the power of God and began calling out people in the audience and giving them prophetic words. The presence of God filled the room, bringing a sense of holy awe to the audience.

This went on for a few minutes, and then David motioned to me and said, "Go ahead." Not sure what to do, I froze, and then I started to panic. There was no way I could do what David was doing, I reasoned. His level and training were way beyond mine. He was a seasoned prophet and an articulate speaker with deep knowledge of church history and Scripture. I was just Hubie, trained in the children's church. My mind went blank, and my insecurities started to flare up. It seemed everyone in the audience was staring at me, which made things even worse. In my mind I was crying out to the Lord, "What do I do now? Help me, please!"

Very distinctly I heard the Holy Spirit answer, "Calm down. I am with you. Just do what you always do. You are not like others, so don't pretend to be." I glanced at David and smiled. A peaceful feeling came over me, and the panic left just as quickly as it had come. I started to walk around the audience and made my way to the back. I walked up to a person and delivered a prophetic word exactly as I usually did. I did the same thing a few more times and then passed it back to David. He prophesied to a few people and then passed the mic back to me. It was as if we were playing a game, handing the mic off to each other. This went on for an hour or so before the meeting came to a close. Many people came up to me afterward saying it was truly amazing to see how two ministers could do the same type of ministry in such different ways. Another person came up and said, "You both ministered in unison. One took the front, and one took the back, and it was interesting to see you both go back and forth. It was so unpredictable. The whole room was covered, when you think about it. I have never seen anything like that before."

It was truly humbling to hear this feedback. I found it amazing that we worked so well together even though we had just met a few minutes before the meeting started. When the session was over, I was fortunate to get to spend a few minutes with David and thank him for all he does. He smiled and thanked me for coming. Easygoing and humble, he carried himself in such a way that you could see he was an extension of the Lord's hand. I thought, "I could learn a lot from this man." As David left, I asked if he would be back, and Mark said he was in town for the conference.

The Lord opened the door for David and me to spend some time together between the conference sessions, and I took advantage of every second with this man of God! I asked him questions and explained how my gift worked and how I began ministering. He looked at me very seriously and said, "You know, Hubie, you are very rare."

I didn't exactly know what he meant, so I said, "Well, I am Korean, Mexican, and American Indian."

He smiled and said, "You are an ecstatic prophet."

Now, where had I heard that before? It was the same thing John Paul Jackson had said!

David continued, "You have bodily functions when you are in prophecy mode. You get sick. Look at Jeremiah; he wept. Look at Ezekiel; his blood boiled. That is you, Hubie!" He then referred me to a book by a woman named Stacey Campbell.

Suddenly everything started to make sense. There was nothing wrong with me; I was just different, and that is OK. God is so creative He doesn't make all of us the same. Ministering throughout the conference, I noticed the people attending looked different from me. Yet when the worship started, we worshipped the same way, to the same God. As I heard a man named Bishop Dale Bronner once say, "We all have the same beliefs, and we are all on the same team." All of us are called to minister, and some of us can do it in different ways, but we all have a common bond, which is our faith in Jesus. No two people are the same, and there is no room in the body of Christ for competition or comparison. In fact, when we lift others up, we lift up ourselves. David and I were examples of this when we ministered together in rhythm, handing off the mic to each other.

After the conference in Australia, I went back home to my family and continued the life of a wandering prophet. Even though I still had some questions, I had more answers than before and kept moving forward using my gift. I now understood that the Lord would provide all the answers I needed in His time through the people He wanted to use. The hardest part of walking with God for me is learning to be patient and waiting for Him to supply all my needs in His timing. I am not the most patient person, but I'm growing and trusting that the Lord knows more than I do.

Lessons Learned Along the Way

As I struggled to patiently wait for the answers I sought, God revealed some significant truths to me during this season of learning about the gift the Lord had given me. I believe they are important for everyone growing in their ministry gift, especially prophetic ministry.

Don't feel pressured to meet or conform to people's expectations.

A person may not be happy with the prophetic word they received. I may not have a prophecy for everyone. Some people try to heighten the experience of meeting a prophet. They expect a prophet to know their whole situation and prophesy an earth-shattering word. I can only speak what the Holy Spirit gives, when He gives it, to whom He gives it. When I get nothing, it's OK. It's OK for me to just be myself, and it's OK for you to just be yourself. You are complete in Christ. Rest in that. Stop feeling pressured to conform to people's expectations as you minister and as you simply live.

God will reveal the answers to your questions about your calling in His perfect timing.

Keep moving forward in the Lord. He reveals things to you on a need-to-know basis. Psalm 119:105 says, "Your word is a lamp to my feet and a light to my path" (MEV). He's not going to reveal everything to you all at once because you may not be ready and wouldn't be able to handle it. Even if God's ways don't make sense to you, remember:

- His thoughts and ways are higher than our thoughts and ways. They are beyond our comprehension, superior, sovereign, and omniscient. Again, Isaiah 55:8 says, "For My thoughts are not your thoughts, nor are your ways My ways, says the LORD" (MEV).

- We can be reassured that He is good and does good. The psalmist wrote, "You are good and do good; teach me Your statutes" (Ps. 119:68, MEV).
- We can calm ourselves down, rest, and put our trust in Him while we wait on the Lord to answer us. Psalm 40:1 says, "I waited patiently for the Lord; and he inclined unto me, and heard my cry."
- We can confidently trust the Lord to lead and guide us in His purposes and assignments while we're waiting for answers. I have seen God's faithfulness to lead me step-by-step in my life. He rarely gives us the whole picture but reveals the next step to take in faith. "A man's heart plans his way, but the Lord directs his steps" (Prov. 16:9). Psalm 37:23 says, "The Lord directs the steps of the godly. He delights in every detail of their lives" (NLT).

If you feel unworthy or inadequate for the call of God in your life, that's actually a good sign.

We must recognize and humbly acknowledge to the Lord that we are indeed inadequate and broken, that we *need* Him. God is not looking for the mighty ones who are self-confident in their own abilities; rather, He appoints the "weak and meek," who place their confidence in God's Spirit and give Him the glory.

Jesus was pretty straightforward when He said we could do nothing without Him:

> Abide in Me, and I in you. As the branch cannot bear fruit of itself, unless it abides in the vine, neither can you, unless you abide in Me. I am the vine, you are the branches. He who abides in Me, and I in him, bears much fruit; for without Me you can do nothing.
>
> —John 15:4–5

The Lord is familiar with all our ways, and He knows that we are broken creatures made of dust (Ps. 103:14). In fact, Jesus, our High Priest in heaven, sympathizes with our weaknesses, and we can draw near to Him in confidence to find help in time of need (Heb. 4:14–16). And He freely gives us wisdom when we ask in faith (Jas. 1:5–6).

It's OK to be scared.

I've been prophesying for more than twenty years, and I still feel scared every single time, up until the moment I open my mouth to prophesy. The Holy Spirit has always been faithful to graciously take over. I think of feeling scared as a check to keep me humble and dependent on the Lord. "God resists the proud, but gives grace to the humble" (Jas. 4:6, MEV).

When the Lord appoints us to a task, He already has prepared the way and equipped us for the work.

The writer of Hebrews prayed that the God of peace would "equip you with everything good for doing his will" and "work in us what is pleasing to him, through Jesus Christ" (Heb. 13:20–21, NIV). God is in control when things go smoothly and even when things don't go as planned. If you feel overwhelmed during a ministry assignment, or if something unexpectedly goes wrong, pause for a moment to be still before God. Wait with expectancy on the Holy Spirit to direct and speak through you. It's OK to pause and pray. We must not feel pressured to get ahead of the Lord or move in our own strength without the Holy Spirit. We can rest in the Lord and have confidence in His Word, which says, "He is the One who goes before you. He will be with you, He will not leave you nor forsake you; do not fear nor be dismayed" (Deut. 31:8).

To help relieve the pressure to live up to people's expectations, remember you are serving the Lord, not man.

Our obedience and allegiance are to God, not man. Our reward comes from Him. "And whatever you do, do it heartily, as to the Lord and not to men, knowing that from the Lord you will receive the reward of the inheritance; for you serve the Lord Christ" (Col. 3:23–24). Not only does our reward come from the Lord, but we are accountable to Him, and "each of us shall give an account of himself to God" (Rom. 14:12, MEV). This should be our motivation.

I described in my first book how my family was hurt by false prophecies. Sometimes people prophesy what they feel instead of by the Spirit of God when they feel pressured to give a word or when they really want to encourage an individual. Though well intended, this behavior is not of God. We can deliver only what the Holy Spirit gives us. Speaking for God is serious business, and we will be held responsible. This is why we should be reluctant prophetic ministers and should never try to make up a prophecy.

Remember, it's OK to be yourself. Let go and put your full faith in God. Let Him lead. He knows more than you do, so you can trust Him and rest as you move forward. The Lord told Moses, "My Presence will go with you, and I will give you rest" (Exod. 33:14). Moses was called to a ministry that was far bigger than he was. He was insecure and felt inadequate, but the Lord was with him. He is with you also, and as long as His presence is going with you, you'll be OK!

Chapter 4

Your Gift Will Make Room for You

WHATEVER YOUR GIFT, it's important to understand that you don't have to force or manipulate it or be opportunistic in any way. If you do, the results can be disastrous. People may receive a prophetic word that gets them off track from God's path. The Lord is faithful and will guide them back but often at the cost of time and unnecessary pain. In addition, a false or ill-timed word can give a person a skewed view of God, especially if the person is a nonbeliever or a new believer without a firm foundation in the Scriptures.

As I briefly mentioned earlier, our family experienced the pain, wrong direction, and other fallout that come from receiving false prophetic words, even though they were given through sincere believers. A person can be quite sincere and still be quite wrong. This is why as prophetic ministers we should always be a little reluctant and move forward with caution—not fear but caution. Typically, but not always, when wrong words are spoken, the people giving the prophecies are sincere but still have wrong or unclear motives. What I mean is, they may really want to encourage you, but they are also looking for affirmation of their gift or the prestige that comes with it. In some cases they also may want to control you and think saying, "Thus says the Lord," gives them more power.

My experience has been that true prophetic ministers are usually a bit reluctant and cautious. They tend to take the approach that they are simply delivering the mail and then remove themselves, letting the Holy Spirit take over. If you are truly called to the prophetic, you don't have to force it or try to make things happen. Your gift will make room for you. Proverbs 18:16 tells us, "A man's gift makes room for him, and brings him before great men" (MEV). No, you don't have to force or manipulate your way. If it's God, He will make a way. We will see this illustrated powerfully in a story later in this chapter. But first, let's see what not to do and then what to do as it relates to letting your gift make room.

What Not to Do

We must be careful to maintain strong, healthy boundaries as we appropriate our giftings, using wisdom to discern motives. Those who force their own gift will use you. This next story is an example of what not to do. It's a lesson in boundaries.

Whenever you're a guest at a church or someone's home,

it is common courtesy to ask permission before doing any prophetic ministry. Personally, I always try to be respectful and obey the house rules when visiting a church or home. I don't want to do anything to disrupt the established order. One time I went to see a pastor friend who was speaking at a church, and while I was there, he introduced me to one of his spiritual sons. We'll call him John. My pastor friend suggested John and I hang out together since we were both prophetic, so we exchanged numbers and then a few texts. Vicki and I were planning a worship gathering at our home, so we invited John over. The plan was for him to stay overnight since we did not know when the occasion would end. He arrived early and helped us get things in order before our guests arrived. Everything was fine until the guests started to arrive.

The doorbell rang, and as I started to go to the door, John raced ahead of me to open it. As the people walked in, John led them to the living room, sat them down, and started to prophesy to them. I was stunned. Unsure of how to react, I just went with it, thinking if it was God's will, I didn't want to judge him. Maybe he was being led by the Holy Spirit for those particular people. About ten minutes later the doorbell rang again, and John did the same thing. He raced to the door and led the couple to the living room and started to prophesy to them. "What is going on?" I thought, starting to get a bit concerned. But once again, instead of reacting, I did nothing.

As John finished talking to that couple, the doorbell rang

again. This time I was standing near the door, so I opened it first and greeted my friends. I politely introduced John to them, and he immediately instructed them to follow him to the living room, where he then directed them to sit down and started to prophesy to them. Now I was really feeling uneasy. After all, this was my home and my guests. I was responsible. When John was done, I told him we needed to talk. He said OK, and the two of us went into another room.

"John," I said in a respectful tone, "do you have prophetic words for everyone who comes through the door?"

"I don't know," he replied.

"If you are certain the Lord is instructing you, then it is fine, but don't you think you should let the guests come in first and at least take off their jackets? We have house rules, and that's just common courtesy."

John looked at me with a blank expression, not knowing how to respond. Apparently that had never occurred to him.

"I don't really know you," I continued, "and I'm not sure how accurate your gift is yet. This is not practice, so don't you think you should ask the host if it's OK to minister to the guests since you are also a guest?"

He nodded but didn't seem to agree.

"If you can't follow the rules, then you can leave," I said. "If you want to minister to anyone, please let me know first, and then we can do it together."

"OK," he said reluctantly, and we left the room.

Later I asked some of the guests John prophesied to how accurate he was. They responded that some of his words were "off"; other parts were ambiguous and could apply to a range of things or people but weren't specific enough to apply to them personally. An example of this would be telling someone she's having financial issues. Well, whether rich or poor, in debt or debt-free, everyone has financial issues. Another example is, "God is moving in your life." This basically applies to everyone. Authentic, Spirit-led prophetic ministry is specific to an individual's situation and calling. Usually prophecies from God are spot-on with pinpoint details, leaving no doubt that they came from Him because there is no way the person delivering the message could have known those details.

No matter how nice a person seems to be, the Scriptures teach that we must "test all things; hold fast what is good" (1 Thess. 5:21). Commentaries on this verse suggest that this testing applies to words prophesied or preached. Such should always be examined by Scripture and judged for accuracy. If a prophetic word does not line up with the Bible, it is not coming from God, regardless of how sweet and nice the person delivering it is. God does not take speaking for Him lightly, and neither should we.

Deuteronomy 12:32 says, "See that you do all I command you; do not add to it or take away from it" (NIV). We must be careful never to add to or subtract from the prophetic word the Holy Spirit gives us for someone. If we do, we could hurt that person, and God will hold us accountable.

I was polite the rest of the night and let John minister to a couple of people as long as I was with him. As I witnessed him giving out "prophetic words," he seemed to be fishing for information and looking for nonverbal cues to determine what he should say next. He seemed to think about what he was saying as if he was adding to whatever the Holy Spirit was telling him. I was trying to justify his actions in my head, and when he finished, I would step in and minister to the people. The night ended, and he left the next morning. He called a few times right afterward and asked if we were having any more get-togethers. I said nothing was on the calendar, and we left it at that.

My whole experience with John that night had left a sour taste in my mouth, and I wasn't sure what the next step was going to be. Some months later he called and asked if I could help him with a business plan since I was a CPA. I told him if he emailed me a copy, I'd look it over and give him my comments. He emailed some raw data and followed up with a phone call. He said he had a meeting with a potential client in a week, and he wanted to know if I could have the business plan done by then.

"I never promised to do it for you," I said. "If you want me to do it, we can talk about a fee."

"You said you would help me," John replied.

"I said I would help you to review it, but I never said I would do it for you. It is a lot of work doing it from scratch, and I would have to schedule time and we would need to discuss a fee."

"Now I am in trouble. I made promises I can't keep. Could you make an exception this time?" John pleaded.

"I'm sorry, but I am busy with my own work," I said. "I just can't."

He got upset, said goodbye, and hung up. I immediately went to pray and ask the Lord if I should help him. I got no answer, which is His way of telling me to just sit tight and do nothing. Another few months passed, and one day a manager from a company I had previously done work for and had a good reputation with called me asking about John. "Your good friend John is here, and we are talking about doing business together," the manager said. "He has told us at the office you both are great friends and that you both minister together."

I was absolutely stunned. John used my reputation and business contact without even consulting me, and then he embellished our relationship. I was furious. I called my business associate at that company and asked him what was going on. He said they were going to prepare a contract with John but wanted to call me first since John and I were such great friends. They were going to give him a contract based upon our friendship. I mentioned that the two of us had only ministered together once and then explained what happened the night he came over to my house for the worship gathering. I also told him we were not close friends, as he had indicated, and it was concerning that he would use my name to further a business relationship with his company. My business associate friend was quiet and at the end replied, "This is unfortunate."

There's another interesting twist to this story. I was

invited to a presidential ball, and toward the end of the night, while I was still ministering there, John showed up. He must have arrived late because I had not seen him earlier and didn't even know he was attending. When John saw me, he immediately wanted to minister with me. I just kept doing what the Holy Spirit was directing me to do. As I ministered to a person, he watched and waited until I was done and had walked away. Then he stepped up to that same person and, I was told, said basically the same thing I did but with different words. My suspicions were confirmed that he'd been simply listening to what came through me and rehashed it, which is not good to do. Unsure of John's motives, I decided to distance myself from him. If he wanted to minister to people, then he should do it away from me, on his own.

I was about to minister to another person and was ready to start when John abruptly interrupted and broke the flow to say he had something to tell them also. Annoyed, I turned around and told him, "Go to the next table and wait for them there."

"Are you kidding?" he responded.

"No. You said you wanted me to train you," I replied. "It is not a good idea that you hear what comes through me. You should be able to do it on your own, so consider this training."

John didn't really have a response, so I repeated what I said: "Go and wait for them at the next table."

I waited until he left and then continued ministering

for about another hour. When finished, I looked over, and John was not there. I asked if anyone saw him, and a woman said he left shortly after going to the other table. This just confirmed his intentions. He was trying to be associated with me to help himself along. John wanted to use my accounting gift and then he tried to use my prophetic gift for his purposes, and I was not going to let him. If the Holy Spirit had directed me to do so, it would have been a different story, but He didn't.

John was an opportunist trying to ride my coattails to manipulate me and use my contacts to further his agenda. He tried to get me to help him by pressuring me to write him a business plan for free when I never agreed to do that. It got frustrating and annoying very fast. I'm mentioning this not to be hard on John but to make you aware that when your gift starts to operate, there will be people who want a piece of you and your gift. They are not there to move you forward but to take what you have and drain you. Be careful. Not everyone around you has the right motives, and not everybody around you is your friend, even when it comes to believers. Yes, you can love them and even try to teach them, but it's critical to have boundaries to protect yourself and keep the gift of God inside you flowing and effective.

That means responding with a strong no at times and distancing yourself. I'm not saying to be mean or rude, but at times to walk effectively in the prophetic, you need the backbone to stand up to people. I have distanced myself from John since his motives did not line up with mine. If you have anyone in your ministry life with a different vision or goal, then it is best to remove yourself from the situation so you will not be distracted.

Again, when you visit churches and homes, it's important that you respect their boundaries when administering the prophetic. John did not respect the house rules. He never asked about the order of worship, prayer, or ministry at the worship gathering at my house. He rushed to prophesy to my guests as soon as they walked through the door, before I had a chance to test the legitimacy and accuracy of his prophetic gift. It was as if he felt he had something to prove. Our aim is never to impress others but to honor and obey God with our ministry gifts.

What to Do

One of my biggest fears when I started my prophetic journey was that I would somehow disappoint the Lord. I took my ministry calling seriously and was extremely cautious to listen and follow His lead when administering the gift. The fear of falling short and misrepresenting the Lord always bothered me, as it should all authentic prophetic ministers.

I once was attending a conference called The Bridge Summit and was ministering to attendees. As the conference was going on, the Lord would highlight certain people to me, and I would watch for the right time to speak to them. I was careful to stay within the boundaries of the conference order and would always wait until an intermission or break, and when the Holy Spirit opened the door, I would walk up to them and speak. Of course, my insecurities were flaring up because the conference was scheduled for three days, and I knew if something went wrong, I would most likely see these people again, and that would be awkward.

During those three days, the Holy Spirit had me busy tapping people and ministering to them. One of the people I had a prophetic word for was a woman named Gretchen Campbell, who was an employee at Bishop Dale Bronner's church, Word of Faith, where the summit was being held. She was in the lobby when the Lord had me speak to her. Gretchen seemed receptive to the word, and the next day, she found me at the conference, tapped me on the shoulder, and said, "My sister would like to speak to you; she's in my office." My first thought was I must have done something wrong. Gretchen was on staff at the church, and now I had to go and see someone in her office. I said, "OK," and followed her. I felt like a sixth-grader being marched by his teacher to the principal's office. Surely this was not going to be good. As we were walking, the negative thoughts raced through my mind. What was this all about? Did I not follow the house rules? Are they going to throw me out? How embarrassing to be taken out of the conference while it was going on.

We arrived at a door, and Gretchen opened it and smiled. I walked in, and there was a woman sitting at a desk. She stood up, reached out her hand, and said, "Hi, I am Courtney Wright." She told me she was the pastor of apostolic ministries at Word of Faith and asked me to sit down, so I sat down and waited to see what happened. I was still unsure of why I was summoned to speak with her. Courtney smiled and said, "I've been watching what you have been doing at the conference." She paused.

My mind raced. "Oh no, here it comes."

She continued, "I have been seeing the effect it has had on the individuals, and it is great. What you are doing is unique and out-of-the-box thinking."

"Thank you," I said, breathing a sigh of relief.

"The prophetic word touched Gretchen, who is my sister, and I just wanted to meet you and say thank you."

I said it was great to be there and thanked her for the excellent job she and her team were doing at the conference. Everything was perfect with all the logistics.

A few months passed, and I received a phone call from Courtney. She said they were having an event for pastors called The Capacity Conference, hosted by Bishop Dale Bronner's church, and she wanted to invite me to it. Courtney said she was thinking out of the box and wanted me to attend, not as a speaker but as an attendee. I wasn't quite sure what she wanted, so I asked her, "You want me to come and not speak but wander around like I did at The Bridge Summit when we met?"

"Yes," she replied. "We would like the prophetic to be present at the conference."

I told her I would pray about it and get back to her. I thought it was an unusual request and a great idea, but I still had to pray about it first. I spent the next few days praying about it, and the Lord said yes, so I called Courtney and accepted the invitation. I wasn't sure how all this was going to work, but I usually just show up, and the Holy Spirit takes it from there.

"You just come and do what you do," Courtney said.

"OK then," I said.

I wasn't exactly sure how I would fit in since I wasn't a pastor and it was a pastors' conference, but as I've said throughout this book, I have learned to be pliable, which is something I've had to continually work on.

I arrived at the conference and recognized a few people but didn't really know anyone. As I began wandering and moving in the prophetic, word spread, and people started to approach me during the breaks—a lot of people. I still wasn't sure how it was all going to work but was trying to be pliable. Early on I had met a guy from Mississippi named Jimmy Lee Wilson, and we hit it off. I knew it was a divine appointment, but I wasn't sure what it was all about yet. When he saw what was going on, he decided to jump in and help.

Jimmy monitored the people and kept order and also allowed me to take breaks when I needed them. He made sure I was attended to when I needed anything. He stayed with me the whole conference. Unlike John, he wasn't out to use me but to be a life giver and helper to me. I never even asked for help, but he jumped in and started to serve. One time when I was taking a break, we had time to chat, and as it turned out, he was a pastor. He said when he saw what was going on, the Lord told him to help me, so he did. It was that simple. Jimmy's humility, quiet confidence, and spirit of servanthood touched me deeply.

As the conference went on, I hardly stopped ministering, but Jimmy was by my side the whole time, keeping things in order and keeping track of the time. The day became a blur due to the constant ministering, but it was all great! I ministered up until the moment it was time to leave. I got home exhausted and poured out, but I knew God's purpose had been accomplished. Jimmy relayed to me that several people told him how encouraged they were. Courtney also called to give me some praise reports that people gave her. As I sat and listened to all the good reports, it was humbling to know God used me as a vessel to help so many people.

And the story doesn't end here. God gave me great favor with Bishop Bronner and Courtney, such that they decided to use my first book, *The Tales of a Wandering Prophet*, as a textbook for a prophecy class they were teaching at the church and even invited me as a guest speaker to minister to the students. And I was invited back to a subsequent Capacity Conference to wander around and do what I do.

My main point is this: God will open the doors for you to administer your prophetic gift in the unique way He created you to minister. God will use your one act of obedience to sovereignly lead you to another open door of opportunity and then another without any need for forced entry on your end or self-promotion.

When You Think You Blew It or Missed a God Appointment

On the last day of the Capacity Conference, I was engaged in conversation with an individual when I noticed a woman in the room and the Holy Spirit nudged me to deliver a prophetic word to her. I continued speaking with the individual for a few minutes, and when I looked up, the woman was gone. Because it was the last day, I rushed outside to look for her. I didn't see her, so I went back into the building and searched some more but did not see her. Waves of disappointment hit me as I realized she was gone. If only I had acted when the Holy Spirit prompted me—if only. But I didn't, and as a result I missed someone who probably needed to hear from Him, someone who probably needed direction, encouragement, or comfort. I had let God and the woman down, and I was feeling regret. One of the guys I was with saw that I looked upset.

"What's wrong?" he asked.

"I was supposed to speak to someone, and I messed up," I said with a dejected look.

"Don't worry," he encouraged me, "no one is perfect, and besides, if you didn't do it, then the Lord will send someone else."

That sounded good, but it didn't really comfort me.

"Hey, let's go eat," he said. "There's a great barbecue place a few miles away."

"OK," I said, forcing a smile. "Barbecue always makes me feel better."

We got into the car and headed to the restaurant. I still felt bad but reasoned there was nothing I could do at that point. As I drove, I asked God for forgiveness, but little did I know, He had a surprise waiting for me. When we entered the doors of the restaurant, to my astonishment the woman was there sitting at a table near the door. I looked at the table, and oddly there was no food or drink on it. I told my friends to go ahead and order because I needed to speak to someone. They laughed and got in line. I walked up to the woman and asked to sit down. She looked up and said, "Please do; I have been waiting for you."

"What?" I said. "What do you mean?"

"I was waiting for you to speak to me at the conference because God told me you would speak to me. After I saw you were busy with a line of people, I left."

I nodded attentively.

"As I was driving home," she continued, "the Holy Spirit told me to go to the barbecue place and just wait, and that's what I'm doing." She obeyed and was just waiting to see what it meant. When she saw me walk in, she laughed, knowing instantly why she was there. "You got something to tell me?" she asked.

I apologized first, and then the prophetic word flowed

out of me. Tears filled her eyes as the word was coming forth. Then a smile spread across her face, and she began to laugh. She became joyful and said thank you so much. She gave me a hug, said thank you again, and left. Once again, I breathed a sigh of relief and thanked the Lord for a second opportunity. The encounter taught me a huge lesson: God is in control. If He wants to get a message to someone, He will do it. And if you have pure motives, the Lord will honor your obedience and even work your perceived mistakes out for His and your good. He wants you to succeed.

I have seen many people through the years who have a prophetic gift, but they stopped walking in it because they felt as if they disappointed God, that they "missed it" or missed a God appointment. They may have been hurt when they were put in a situation and didn't perform the way they thought they should have, so they just quit. But as this story played out, if you are trying to be obedient, God will direct your steps to correct your course when necessary. Relax. "Trust in the LORD, and do good; dwell in the land, and feed on His faithfulness" (Ps. 37:3).

At times, you may receive a word, a knowing, or an instruction from God and feel as if you don't know what to do next or as if you missed an appointment. You may feel as though you failed God. If this happens, don't give up. Instead, take a step back. God could be teaching you how to hear His voice by giving you a foreshadowing of something in the future. A lot of people actually get upset by thinking that they messed up when in reality God simply intended for them just to understand how He speaks to them. It's the Holy Spirit showing you how He talks to you so you can have confidence in your relationship with Him. You'll know it was Him because what He told you will come to pass. It's incorrect to assume that you have to deliver everything the Holy Spirit speaks to you. He may be giving you insight into a situation or showing you information about a person so you can intercede in prayer. Not everything He shows and tells you requires immediate action.

Trust God to Open the Doors

To recap what we've been discussing in this chapter, I want to encourage you to remember the following:

Exercise discernment and set healthy boundaries.

Be prayerful and careful about whom you associate with, even if someone appears nice and comes highly recommended from someone you trust.

Be careful not to manipulate or be opportunistic.

If it is God, you don't have to force things. What I have seen happen time and time again in my own ministry is the Lord sends me to the right place at the right time to speak to the right person. God needs neither our help nor our agenda. We should not try to ride someone's coattails, nor should we allow others to ride our coattails, to reach the destiny God has assigned for us or them. The only exception is mentorship. If God has assigned you to mentor someone, then you should train that person and in time allow him or her to minister alongside you and learn from you.

You're unique, so be yourself.

Though I mentioned this in an earlier chapter, I feel this needs to be reinforced. The only way to maximize your effectiveness when exercising your gift is to be the unique person God created and called you to be. If you try to be someone else by caving in to pressure or conforming to expectations, whether your own or others', you will be out of alignment with God and hinder His flow during ministry.

If you are sincerely trying to be obedient to God, rest assured in His promise to lead you and direct your path.

The Lord is trustworthy even when He tells you to do something that doesn't make sense to you. "Trust in the LORD with all your heart, and lean not on your own understanding; in all your ways acknowledge Him, and He will direct your paths" (Prov. 3:5–6, MEV). He is sovereign and in control of all things, so nothing happens by chance or without His foreknowledge. If you believe you have failed Him or feel stuck, He already foreknew that would happen. Yet He still chooses and equips us to be carriers of His word.

The apostle Peter failed Jesus by denying Him three times before the rooster crowed. Jesus knew all along Peter would fail Him and told him so (Matt. 26:33–35). After Jesus was crucified, Peter was dejected and had given up, but when the resurrected Jesus encountered him, He told Peter, "Feed My sheep." (See John 21:16–18.) Jesus knows all things. He knew Peter would fail Him, and He knew Peter loved Him. Peter's failure did not disqualify him. Neither does yours. The Lord has already accounted for our every failure and misstep when He directs our path. Nothing can thwart His purposes. "I know that You can do everything," said Job, "and that no purpose of Yours can be withheld from You" (Job 42:2).

Let us follow Jesus' example to hear and speak only what God tells us to speak, no more and no less.

Jesus submitted Himself to the Father's authority concerning what to say and do. He said, "Truly, truly, I say to you, the Son can do nothing of Himself, unless it is something He sees the Father doing" (John 5:19, NASB). Likewise, when Jesus spoke concerning the promised Holy Spirit, He said the Holy Spirit would disclose to us only what He hears from Jesus Himself:

> But when He, the Spirit of truth, comes, He will guide you into all the truth; for He will not speak on His own, but whatever He hears, He will speak; and He will disclose to you what is to come.
>
> —JOHN 16:13, NASB

The prophetic gift is something I take very seriously with fear and trembling because I am representing God. My desire is to serve Him and please Him, but I do not want to misrepresent Him in any way. I am reluctant and have completely removed myself from the equation so I can know without a doubt that when I speak, the Holy Spirit is directing me. This should be your goal too as you move forward in your prophetic gift.

Establishing good boundaries for ourselves and others is critical. We don't have to manipulate or force our gift, nor should we let others do so to us. God is in control and able. If He has called you, your gift will make room for you.

Chapter 5

Church Hurt

TO MOVE FREELY in the prophetic, God needs an unhindered vessel. While He can speak through a donkey, He prefers people. Human beings are the conduit through which the Holy Spirit moves most of the time. It's the way God set it up. In Acts 21 we see a prophet named Agabus, who spoke a word to Paul. Before Paul left for a trip to Jerusalem, Agabus grabbed him by the belt and said, "Thus says the Holy Spirit, 'So shall the Jews at Jerusalem bind the man who owns this belt, and deliver him into the hands of the Gentiles'" (Acts 21:11). Though it wasn't the most encouraging of words, it was the Holy Spirit speaking prophetically through Agabus.

The Holy Spirit is still speaking prophetically through people today. However, for Him to speak consistently through us, we must stay connected to and in tune with the still, small voice of the Holy Spirit. We must also be unobstructed vessels. "Since we live by the Spirit," wrote

Paul, "let us keep in step with the Spirit" (Gal. 5:25, NIV). This scripture clearly shows that it is possible to live by the Spirit, which is being born-again, yet not keep in step with the Spirit. Stepping out in the prophetic requires keeping in step with the Holy Spirit, and that means keeping our connection free of interference or distractions that can interrupt the flow of His voice.

If you are serious about walking in the prophetic flow, you must also be serious about keeping your life clear of hindrances. One of the things that hinder our flow is obviously sin. A person can't be knowingly living in sin and still expect to hear God clearly. As with Balaam, whose donkey spoke when Balaam would not listen to the Lord (Num. 22:21–39), God can use us despite us, but it is usually for a short time. This is why you see some ministries start out strong, even grow big and do powerful works, only to crash and burn in the end. All spiritual leaders, including those who walk in the prophetic, must maintain their openness before God.

Most of us know 1 John 1:9: "If we confess our sins, He is faithful and just to forgive us our sins and to cleanse us from all unrighteousness." John was talking to Christians. Open fellowship is maintained with God as we continue walking in the light that He reveals to us. Confession and repentance of sin are the way to find restoration and unbroken fellowship with God. They cleanse the conscience and remove every obstacle from communion with Christ.

Yet there are other, more subtle things that block our flow that the Lord will shine His light on. They are unresolved hurt and unforgiveness, strongholds from our past that keep us blocked even if we don't know it. God gave me a wake-up call regarding the bitterness and unforgiveness still in my heart, though I thought they were gone.

Vicki and I both grew up in broken, dysfunctional homes. When we first got married, we clung to each other, but we also felt the need to be part of a family because neither of us experienced the love and affirmation children should receive from their parents. We were wounded, backslidden twenty-four-year-olds when we started our married life together and vowed that we would be the opposite of what we experienced growing up. Six months into our journey, both of us were jolted to our cores when we were involved in a horrific car accident that could have killed or severely injured us. Seeing how God had supernaturally protected our lives set us back on the path of seeking Him for our future.

Over the next eighteen months, we visited church after church. Baptist, Episcopalian, Presbyterian, Methodist—it didn't matter what label or denomination; all we wanted was a biblically sound fellowship we could call home. The Holy Spirit answered our prayers by leading us to a full-gospel congregation that would become our church family for the next fourteen years. We were happy we found a home! The pastor was like a parent to us. We fellowshipped and bonded over family meals, at church picnics, and on missionary trips. We helped each other out when in need and even started families at the same time. One year, eight women gave birth to babies in the span of a few months! Our desire to be part of a family was met at this church, and we were growing in our spiritual walk, so we were quite content. We never imagined that one day the Holy Spirit would tell us to leave.

About a year before we left, a rapid string of false prophecies spoken over our family, as well as some obvious signs of control and manipulation by the church leadership, opened our eyes to some issues we had not seen before. We were disturbed but still loved our church family. However, the Holy Spirit told us it was time to leave, so we reluctantly obeyed. Back then we did not understand how God works in seasons to lead us from one place to the next in His divine timing for His divine purposes.

Wanting to leave the right way, we wrestled with how to inform the pastor, who had been like a parent to us. Also, knowing our absence would have a negative financial impact on this small church distressed us greatly. To our utter shock and dismay, instead of encouraging us to obey the Spirit's leading, the pastor, church leadership, and many of the church members shunned us and made false accusations that were extremely hurtful. The people we called our friends and family, whom we had so desperately clung to, stopped speaking to us and treated us as rebellious outcasts. Deeply hurt and disillusioned, we retreated to our home like bleeding soldiers to tend our wounds. "Well, we have each other and our children, and that's all we need," Vicki and I reasoned in an attempt to comfort each other.

After a year of self-imposed isolation at home, we sensed we needed to return to a fellowship of believers but were feeling gun-shy about going to a new church. I searched the local phone book and internet for an Assemblies of God church and found one only five minutes from where we lived. "Let's start here," I convinced Vicki. It was a small church, and we felt right at home from the moment we walked in. Everyone was so nice, so I asked the Lord, "Is this the place You have for us?" I got no reply, so we kept attending. I have learned if there is no answer from God, then I don't do anything different if I can help it.

A few weeks later Pastor Mike Shahid invited us over to his house for a picnic. We had such a great time eating, chatting, and worshipping with him and some other people from the church that I started to think this could be the next place for us to call home. However, as I was praying later that evening, the Holy Spirit whispered, "This is not the place for you, but stay in contact with Pastor Mike."

Not completely understanding God's purpose for telling us this was not to be our church home, we started church hunting again, but I did not mention it to Pastor Mike just yet. I wanted to take it slowly and carefully because of the way we were treated when we left the other church. When that day arrived, I was expecting the worst outcome, but I was hopeful for the best. "The Lord is directing us to another church," I told Pastor Mike apprehensively, "but I would like to remain friends and stay in contact." To my surprise, Pastor Mike smiled warmly and replied, "Whatever God wants."

"I'm sorry; I feel bad about it," I told him.

"There is nothing to be sorry about," he reassured me.

I left the meeting feeling a bit sad because I liked Pastor Mike a lot. He was such a godly, authentic man who cared about people, and his reaction to the news of our departure was the complete opposite of what we had previously experienced. So I concluded that it is possible to leave a church on good terms and decided to forgive those who had hurt Vicki and me. It was time to let go of the bitterness, forget the past, and move forward. I was over it! Or so I thought. Little did I realize the Lord was about to reveal to me that the hurt and bitterness I thought I'd let go of were actually hidden deep in my heart.

An Unexpected Realization

A few weeks later I flew across the country to Redding, California, for a weeklong meeting with accounting clients who also happened to be former members of the church that had shunned us. All week the Holy Spirit brought to surface the unforgiveness and bitterness I had been convinced I was over but in reality had only buried deep inside my heart. As the toxic feelings rose up in me, I could no longer live in denial and was forced to deal with them.

The Holy Spirit began working on my heart at dinner one night with my client friends as our discussion took a turn from accounting to the issues with the church that we had all left. The difference was they were somehow able to leave on good terms, whereas Vicki and I had left on bad terms, no matter how hard we tried to do it right. The conversation was getting intense when one of the men turned to me and said, "You know, Hubie, you're really not over it yet."

Stunned, I replied, "What do you mean? I am so over the way we were treated."

"Um, no, you are not," he responded. I disagreed with him again, so we just dropped the subject and hung out.

The next night, I met a man at dinner named Iain Bradbeer, whom God would use to help me see I really wasn't over my church hurt. My client friend introduced me to Iain and told him about my prophetic gift. Iain was a teacher in the prophetic, so he asked me about my background, the church I attended, and how I learned about the prophetic. I told him the story of how the Lord had divinely orchestrated a meeting between Vicki and her coworker to lead us to the full-gospel church, where we stayed for fourteen years, and everything we learned there, from Spirit-led worship to serving on missionary trips. I told him that my prophetic gift began on a missionary trip to Sweden with a group from that church.

What I conveniently left out were the details of how it all ended badly when we left. Still, the Holy Spirit gave me a word for Iain, and I prophesied over him. He was so overcome by the presence of God that he fell back and slid off the barstool onto the floor! Iain taught a prophecy class at Bethel Church in Redding, and he invited me to attend the class the next morning. I accepted but wasn't prepared for what God had in store for me. The Holy Spirit was about to dig deeper to clean out the hidden hurts I had buried in my heart.

The next morning, as I entered the classroom, Iain pulled out a chair and placed it in the middle of the classroom and asked me to sit in it. He did not tell the students anything about me before he called them to come pray and prophesy over me. The presence of the Holy Spirit was very strong. After they finished, Iain asked for the name of the church I used to attend. I told him the name, and he wrote it on a piece of paper on an easel, along with a timeline of the major events I had experienced at the church, including the point when I started prophesying. He then instructed the students, "Everybody, let's get up and start praising God for the fact that this church took Hubie off the street, where he was, all the way to the point where he started prophesying, and look at what's happened to him now! Let's thank God for this church because if it hadn't been for them, who knows where Hubie would be now!"

"Praise God! Hallelujah!" shouted the students as they started dancing around the room and around me while I sat in the chair feeling bewildered by the commotion. Then they started praying for the church and the church members.

"What are they doing?" I thought. "Why are they doing this? I don't want to pray for them! They don't deserve to be prayed for. After all, they treated us so badly." These condemning thoughts popped into my mind at rapid fire as I silently objected to the ministry happening around me. Now the anger and bitterness in my heart began bubbling to the surface. Feeling as if I were about to erupt, I wanted to tell the students to stop but didn't. Then, while I was sitting there simmering, something happened. There was a shift in the room's atmosphere. You might call it supernatural. After about ten minutes or so, as the hallelujahs and praises echoed around me, the loving conviction of the Holy Spirit fell on me, and my eyes were opened.

"What am I thinking? Why am I so angry at them?" Overcome by remorse, I recalled how the Lord had led Vicki to the church and then I soon followed. Precious memories of all the missionary trips and other events where God had shown up filled my mind. Our time there had been a fourteen-year journey of trials and victories that grew us to our current walk of faith. Oh, how much I had learned over the years. Right before my eyes my bitterness was somehow morphing into gratefulness, and I was now actually missing all those people who had once been a family to us. All I had dwelled upon was the hurt and pain of leaving. It never occurred to me to ask myself, "What if the church never existed or had not been in our path?"

My eyes became moist, and the more I thought about it, the more emotional I became. Then a floodgate burst open, releasing the tears and the pressure. I wept. And when I realized my role in all this, I wept even harder. Until that breaking point, I had been in denial of my bitterness and pain. Instead of resolving the issue and forgiving them, as I thought I had, I just conveniently "forgot" and tried to move on. I had simply put a bandage on an open wound rather than doing the necessary treatment for complete healing to occur. As the Holy Spirit brought this illumination to my soul, right there I asked the Lord to forgive me for my hardened heart, and then I began to pray for the church and the people I once considered family. I wholeheartedly forgave them that day, and I have been able to move forward ever since. Every now and then the memories of us leaving pop up, but they do not bother me anymore. The sting is gone. The Holy Spirit's healing was final.

Lessons in Letting Go

My time with Iain's prophecy class taught me that if you can't pray for a person or group, it's a clear sign you're not over your issues with them. Many times instead of reconciling the issue we push it deep down into our hearts and attempt to forget about it. Unfortunately it remains buried there just waiting for an opportune time to pop back out and sting us. Usually it's when we are least expecting it. This burying of an issue often happens because of denial, when we have a hard time accepting the fact that the offense occurred. Or we want to avoid confrontation, so we play the avoidance game. This doesn't make the issue disappear; it only delays the inevitable.

People can't really go forward in the fullness God has for them until they reconcile the past through genuine repentance and forgiveness. Unforgiveness and bitterness keep us stuck. Forgiveness, however, sets us free, whether or not reconciliation is possible. Forgiveness prevents the devil from getting a foothold in our hearts, which will affect our walk with God, our ability to hear from Him, and our ability to minister to people.

James 1:20 tells us, "For the wrath of man does not produce the righteousness of God." Allowing anger and bitterness to simmer inside us never produces righteousness in us. Proverbs 19:11 says, "The discretion of a man makes him slow to anger, and his glory is to overlook a transgression." It couldn't be plainer. The ability to forgive brings God's glory on a person. Paul summed it up this way:

> Therefore, putting away lying, "Let each one of you speak truth with his neighbor," for we are members of one another. "Be angry, and do not sin": do not let the sun go down on your wrath, nor give place to the devil....And be kind to one another, tenderhearted, forgiving one another, even as God in Christ forgave you.
>
> —EPHESIANS 4:25–27, 32

> If it is possible, as much as depends on you, live peaceably with all men.
>
> —ROMANS 12:18

These passages make clear that holding on to unforgiveness hurts us more than the person who hurt us. Someone wise once said, "Holding on to unforgiveness and bitterness is like drinking poison and expecting the other person to die." That's true.

As Vicki and I have shared our journey to forgive, several questions have come up repeatedly.

What if it's hard for me to forgive someone because of repeated offenses?

There are two ways Vicki and I have dealt with this, according to Matthew 18:21–22:

> Then Peter came to Him and said, "Lord, how often shall my brother sin against me, and I forgive

> him? Up to seven times?" Jesus said to him, "I do not say to you, up to seven times, but up to seventy times seven."

I have to say before I go any further that forgiveness like this is impossible without the grace and power of God. We can't do it on our own. In some situations Vicki and I have been able to overlook repeated offenses by choosing not to get offended because the Holy Spirit revealed to us the condition of that person's heart and imparted His compassion to us to pray for that person. When Jesus was hanging on the cross, unfairly accused, He cried out, "Father, forgive them, for they do not know what they do" (Luke 23:34). In other situations the act of forgiveness becomes a process, a daily choice toward obedience that we make despite our feelings.

This was the case for Vicki when she was repeatedly hurt by someone close to her over many years. I will call that person Anne. Vicki had rehearsed a speech in her mind to one day tell Anne of all the ways she had been hurt by her. Vicki wanted to be obedient to God in forgiving Anne but lacked the desire to do so because she was angry and bitter at Anne's ongoing behavior. So Vicki began to pray this prayer daily for years: "Father, You know my heart and how I feel about this person. I want to do the right thing before Your eyes, but I am unable to forgive this person in my own strength. You know I don't want to do it, so I ask the Holy Spirit to do the work of forgiveness inside of me and for me. Today I choose, as an act of my will, to forgive Anne for ____________. Thank You, Holy Spirit, for doing it. Amen."

Vicki did not think or feel any differently after saying this prayer, but she continued to repeat it every day for over twenty years. Think about that for a minute. Twenty years. Working through these types of issues is often a long-term process. Then it happened.

One day Vicki received an unexpected phone call from Anne. She was crying hysterically, begging for forgiveness. "Finally, this is my chance to vent and tell Anne everything she's done to me over the years," Vicki thought as she listened to Anne explain why she had behaved so badly toward her. As Vicki opened her mouth to unleash her well-rehearsed speech, the Holy Spirit seized her tongue so none of those condemning words could be released. Three times she tried to speak to no effect. "That's OK, I forgive you," Vicki finally whispered, astonished as she listened to her own voice utter these words.

At that moment, Vicki realized what the Holy Spirit had done. He had completed the work of forgiveness in her heart, and the bitterness was replaced with compassion for Anne. Since that day, Vicki and Anne have repaired and deepened their relationship in ways Vicki never thought were possible.

Why is a break in relationship with a church or church member so painful?

If you love somebody like a family member, a rift causes much more pain and offense. Also, Christians often have higher expectations of other Christians, so their disappointment is more severe when expectations are unmet. Putting your best effort into doing something the right way and then being rejected can be deflating. It makes you want to retreat to a safe place and just hide, to give up on people and relationships. It seems as if it's not worth the effort or pain.

In some situations the offender may be doing what is right in his own eyes when he cannot see eye to eye with you. Vicki and I have learned not to place expectations on people because it's easy to be disappointed and tempted to cast judgment when our expectations are unmet. When an issue arises or a promise is broken, we say, "It is what it is," and try to stay levelheaded as we ask God to help us deal with it. The only person we have expectations of is God, according to Psalm 39:7, which says, "And now, Lord, what do I wait for? My hope is in You." And Psalm 62:5 says, "My soul, wait silently for God alone, for my expectation is from Him."

Why did the relationship go bad if I was being obedient to God by attending this church?

Vicki and I have learned to rely on the Holy Spirit to lead us to the church He wants us to attend in a given season because He has purpose in it. It has nothing to do with our personal preferences, our like or dislike of the people, or whether we feel we fit in. And we stay until the Holy Spirit tells us it's time to leave. God has allowed us to experience both highs and lows in all the churches we've attended, training us and instructing us to serve the believers who are there. Nothing we experienced, whether good or bad, was in vain because God has purpose in allowing trials, hardship, and pain to refine our character. There is no perfect church, and unfortunately pain is part of the equation in relationships. Yet it's easy to forget the good and remember the bad. And if things end badly, it tends to have a deeper impact because it's more recent and painful. I remember my former pastor used to say, "It's not important how you started; what's important is that you finish strong."

As Vicki and I received healing and moved forward, we were able to help other former members from this church heal and move forward. We've also helped bring healing to people who've been hurt in other churches. As I pointed out at the beginning of this chapter, to be an effective vessel of God, you need to be unobstructed and pure. This can be very hard. If you feel triggered and get distracted, the memories come back. But harboring pain and unforgiveness blocks the flow of the Holy Spirit and hinders you from ministering. Harboring unforgiveness pits us against someone else and causes division when in actuality we are all on the same team.

The ultimate goal for us and those we are ministering to prophetically is to grow in Christlikeness. Each of us is on a different spiritual level and path. Walking in the prophetic gift allows the Holy Spirit to speak not only to others but also to us and our issues. To be unobstructed, we must allow ourselves to be healed through the pain, lessons, and purification process God brings into our lives. Don't bury your wounds, letting them simmer inside you, and remain unhealed. That will only hinder you and delay you from moving forward.

Chapter 6

Lost and Found

How do we help those who are lost or backslidden find their way back to God? How do we help those who are struggling with life come into alignment with their purpose? Should we speak or let our actions be our testimony? Should we leave the door open or cut them off? These are hard questions to answer, especially when that person is a close friend, a loved one such as a spouse, a wayward child, or even a parent.

One of the primary ways God uses the prophetic is to bring His lost or wandering children back to Him. Yet each individual is at a different place in life and has unique needs and wounds. Part of walking in the prophetic is learning when to confront and when to be silent, when to embrace people and when to release them. It's learning to discern if someone is taking advantage of us or is really in need. We love, yes. And we serve. But we cannot fix or rescue people, nor should we. That is God's job. He will use the stress and difficulties in people's lives to cause them to cry out to Him so He can show up for them. We are not God. Knowing what to do for others and when takes the Holy Spirit's wisdom over our natural wisdom. Recognizing the difference between the Lord's wisdom and our own requires being in tune with the Holy Spirit, as we discussed in the previous chapter.

There is an astounding passage of Scripture in Acts chapter 16 that speaks to this issue. It says, "Now when they had gone through Phrygia and the region of Galatia, they were forbidden by the Holy Spirit to preach the word in Asia" (v. 6). Paul, Silas, and Timothy were forbidden to preach the Word, God's truth. Why would the Holy Spirit tell them not to share the Word of God somewhere? Aren't we supposed to shout it from the rooftops and tell everyone we meet? Apparently not. Why? Because the Holy Spirit knows things we don't and is orchestrating in ways beyond our understanding.

This principle is true on a global level and on an individual level, especially in relationships. There is a time the Holy Spirit wants us to speak, and there is a time He wants us to remain silent. There is a time to be tough and a time to be sympathetic. Something else important to note here is, while some have the gift of prophecy, all believers have the Holy Spirit inside them, who prompts, nudges, and guides. He even speaks prophetically at times through us in our relationships, including relationships with those close to us. The Lord taught Vicki and me this firsthand when we were walking through difficult seasons with our son Daniel and our friend George. He even gave us a surprising prophetic word.

Lessons From Home

Vicki and I were overjoyed when our first child, Sara, was born and then our son Daniel arrived seventeen months later. As first-time parents, we couldn't have asked for an easier baby to raise than Sara. Obedient, even-tempered, and independent, she predictably met every milestone described in Dr. Spock's baby-care book. Daniel, on the other hand, was the complete opposite. Bighearted but opinionated, he marched to the beat of his own drum. In Asian culture, children are expected to achieve straight A's in school and graduate to become doctors, lawyers, or engineers. Not Daniel. As a creative, hands-on learner, he was wired differently and didn't come close to fitting any of those molds. If you look up the phrase *think outside the box* in the dictionary, you may even find a picture of Daniel beside it! All this led to boredom in school, where he stubbornly refused to follow rules. We tried everything we knew to deal with him—positive reinforcement and punishment. Neither had any effect.

Vicki and I were at our wits' end and didn't know what to do. This challenge was bigger than us, and we feared for his future. Looking back, we made many mistakes. Comparing Daniel with our other children was one. Instead of appreciating and nurturing his unique, God-given makeup, we were disappointed he didn't meet our expectations. Yet, despite our shortcomings as parents, God was faithful and was working in Daniel as well as Vicki and me.

As Daniel grew, he developed severe eczema across his entire body. This is a condition that causes painful rashes, along with swelling and dry, cracked skin. When it's severe, as in Daniel's case, there is intense itching combined with a burning sensation. It made him miserable and also looked awful at times. As a result, he got bullied in school and felt like an outcast. This only added fuel to the fire of his rebellion. In angry, bitter protest he would yell, "Life isn't fair!" There is no pain like watching your child suffer, and we hurt for our son. Yet we were powerless to change his situation.

Both the sickness and bullying planted negative seeds in his heart that grew into full-blown cynicism toward the world. Though the Lord would ultimately heal Daniel's eczema, his suffering and mistreatment left deep emotional scars. Daniel was frustrated and hurting and in desperate need of healing in his soul. "You are right, son, life isn't fair," I would tell him. "But you must understand that no one is exempt from suffering. It is part of life, and how you respond to it is what counts."

No matter what I said or how much I tried to encourage him, I was rejected. Nothing, it seemed, could break through Daniel's victim mentality. Even worse, the anger within him grew uncontrollable, to the point where being around him was like maneuvering through a minefield. One unintentional misstep would trigger an explosive argument. We never knew what to expect. This was a dark period for our family, filled with tension and strife that spilled over into family holidays and vacations. What happened to our sweet boy with the heart of gold? Though we would later understand that God was working, we couldn't see it initially. It was difficult being a servant of the Lord while feeling the constant prick of your child's pain and being powerless to fix it.

Daniel eventually graduated high school and decided to move to California to attend a ministry school. We were disappointed he chose not to attend college but felt God led him there and were relieved the house felt peaceful once again. The fact that he chose to attend a ministry school showed us that at his core he still believed in God, and this gave us hope that God would somehow turn his life around. Daniel stayed in California after graduation with no intention of moving back home, and as sad as it is to admit, I was glad he stayed. Seeing him every day used to remind me of my failures as a father, but now he was out of sight and out of mind unless there was an issue he needed my help with.

Struggling to make a living, Daniel survived on a steady diet of protein powder and eggs. We could tell he'd lost weight when we spoke to him through a video app. Vicki was heartbroken, but I told myself it was his choice to live this way. Vicki grew increasingly concerned, so one day she came to me and said, "We need to pray for Daniel to come home." I looked at her with a blank stare and asked, "Why? He made a choice, so let him learn and grow up. Besides, he doesn't want to come home." Being selfish, all I could imagine was the peace and quiet being replaced by stress and fighting if he moved back home.

Vicki approached me again after a few days, this time with an expression that let me know she meant business, and she said with a stern voice, "We need to pray our baby home!" Vicki was on a mission now. Usually when something rises up in her like this, it means she must have heard from God. My choice was either stand my ground or trust my wife. I decided to trust my wife, but I really wasn't 100 percent on board. We started to pray earnestly and boldly for Daniel to come home, even though I didn't desire it. Over time, however, the Lord began changing my mind as well as my heart. Maybe things would be different this time, I reasoned.

Our prayers started being answered when Daniel came home for a visit at Christmastime. Then, to my surprise, one day the Holy Spirit gave me a nudge that He had a word for Daniel. I knew it didn't come from me when He said to Daniel, "The Lord says to come home and everything you're searching for is here in New Jersey." Daniel grudgingly moved back home about six months later. And when he did, all my worst fears came true. Vicki had heard from God, and Daniel had received and obeyed a prophecy confirming he should come home, but instead of peace our home was again filled with strife. I didn't know what else to do at this point but ride it out. I would soon learn the Holy Spirit would use this time to develop His fruit of patience in all of us.

At first, nothing seemed to go right for Daniel. He was fired from jobs or was a disgruntled employee or couldn't make any friends and saw no value in attending community college. It appeared we had missed it and the word was off, so he blamed God and us for encouraging him to leave the community he loved in California. As a concerned parent, I kept offering him advice because I wanted him to avoid the same mistakes I had made. One day he angrily shot back, "If I want your advice, I will ask for it!" Ouch! I was offended and hurt by his response, but it caused me to look at the exchange from his point of view, and when I did, I realized my advice was falling on deaf ears because it was interpreted as nagging and my telling him what to do.

Being a direct person and problem solver, I thought I was helping by giving him the answers to his problems, but I was actually driving Daniel further away. This taught me a big lesson about the power of perception and having sympathy. I needed to back off, try to put myself in his shoes to see how he was perceiving things, and adjust how I communicated with him. If there was any hope of the wall between us breaking down, it was going to be God's doing and not mine. My job now was to let go, love my son, and trust the Lord with Him.

It was heart-wrenching to stand on the sidelines and watch Daniel learn from his mistakes, but sure enough, his decisions had consequences. Whenever he mentioned to me the issues he was facing, I would remark, "Yeah, that happened to me too." If he didn't ask me to share more, I stayed silent. After a while Daniel started to realize perhaps his dad did know something after all. Then one day he approached me and said, "If you have advice, ask me if I want it first." I wish I could tell you I was the understanding, agreeable father who said, "That's wonderful, son," but something in Daniel's tone rubbed me wrong, and pride rose up in me, clouding my judgment. I was offended and rudely blurted, "No, son, you will figure it out," and stomped away.

While I was feeling angry and upset in my bedroom, the Holy Spirit's conviction pierced me. I was Daniel's father, and he was my son, a young man whom I truly loved, but I was the one acting like an immature child. This was Daniel's way of reaching out for help, and I had rejected him. Sitting there in my bedroom, I recalled the parable of the lost sheep and how Jesus, the Good Shepherd, had pursued the lost. He would not hesitate to leave the ninety-nine to pursue that one lost and wandering sheep (Luke 15:4–6). Daniel's soul wasn't lost. He was saved, but he had lost his way in life, or had not found it yet. He was definitely out of alignment, and I could help.

I was so anguished that I rushed downstairs to tell Daniel how sorry I was and ask for his forgiveness. Both of us agreed to respect each other, and Daniel gave me permission to point out things when I saw them, if I gave him the opportunity to accept or reject my advice. This was the breakthrough moment in our relationship. Since that day, Daniel has grown to trust my judgment, and now I'm free to speak into his life. He even seeks my opinion on different matters before making a decision. Fast-forward to today. Daniel is walking with God and realizing his dreams as an audio engineer and music producer right here in New Jersey, just as the prophetic word had said. And having once had a strained relationship, we became very close. God is faithful!

Closer Than a Brother

George was in a bad mood the day we met because he had been wearing the same clothes for three days. He had flown into New Jersey for work and was staying at the home of a mutual friend when we came to visit. His meetings were already finished, but he couldn't leave because the airline had lost his luggage and promised to deliver it to our friend's house. Neither of us knew at the time that his being stuck at the house waiting for his lost luggage was all part of a divine setup for us to meet and become close friends.

George and I introduced ourselves, and then he quickly excused himself to make a call in the basement. I felt that familiar nudge of the Holy Spirit and sensed I needed to follow him to the basement. "You want me to follow him downstairs?" I asked the Lord. "That's a bit weird since we just met, but OK, Lord." I got up from the sofa and started praying as I nervously made my way down to the basement. "What am I doing?" I mumbled under my breath. "He's going to think I'm a stalker. What am I going to say to him when I get downstairs?" Then I remembered there is a bathroom in the basement, so I could just say I had to use it. Yes, that was my excuse!

When I reached the bottom of the stairs, George was standing in the hallway by the bathroom with his back to me, speaking on the phone and sounding very upset. I was headed toward the bathroom when the Holy Spirit unexpectedly steered me to walk up behind him and place my hand firmly on his shoulder. It didn't make sense, but I went with it. George turned around and gave me a dead stare. I cracked a weak smile and said, "I have to go to the bathroom," as I removed my hand from his shoulder and slipped past him. I quickly shut the bathroom door behind me as a myriad of anxious thoughts raced through my mind. "God, what did I just do? Why did I place my hand on his shoulder? What is this guy going to think? And what if he tells my friend? What is my friend going to think?"

I took a deep breath, composed myself, and exited the bathroom, but George was no longer in the hallway. How strange that God would have me follow a stranger to the basement just to put my hand on his shoulder. I walked back up the stairs to the living room and sat down. I glanced at George, and he smiled back, so I assumed all was OK. He told me later that he went to the basement to call the airline for an update on his luggage. No wonder he sounded upset.

My friend had invited Vicki and me to his house that particular evening to lead worship for one of his small-group gatherings. We had a beautiful time in God's presence, singing, praying, and prophesying to all the people there, including George, who would not have been there had it not been for his lost luggage. Right when the gathering ended, at around midnight, the doorbell rang. It was the airline courier delivering George's lost luggage. Talk about timing! Vicki and I felt as if we had made a connection with George, so we exchanged contact information and agreed to keep in touch.

Memorial Day was coming up, and we had no plans, so we decided to invite George over for the long weekend. We had a great time. The kids bonded with him, and he instantly became part of the family. It was then that George brought up the shoulder incident. He told us that he was so aggravated with the airline over the delay in delivering his luggage that he was about to give an earful to the agent on the phone, but when I placed my hand on his shoulder, he immediately felt a calm release that all was going to be OK regarding his luggage, so he refrained. Once again, the Holy Spirit reassured me that I was hearing from Him and He could be trusted even in the little, and sometimes weird, nudges.

Over the next few years, George would fly in to visit, and we kept in touch on a regular basis. His hilarious jokes and spot-on impersonations filled our house with laughter. The kids even called him their godfather. This was a special relationship. He became the brother I wished I'd had growing up, and God also led me to mentor George in his prophetic gifting. He discovered it a few months before we met, but I could tell it was strongly anointed and accurate. I even invited George to minister alongside me to help him build his confidence and practice prophesying. What a blessing it was to see George so on fire to serve the Lord!

Then we noticed George started distancing himself from us. He stopped visiting, and the phone calls became sporadic and superficial. Clearly an emotional wall was being erected between us by our dear brother. We were hurt and didn't know what we had done. Soon, however, it became obvious that George had distanced himself from us because he had distanced himself from God and had lost his zeal. Now things started to make sense. It was agonizing to watch someone we loved, who had walked along the straight and narrow, shaken by life's issues and decide to take a wrong turn. Our beloved family member had gone astray, and we didn't know when or if he would return to the Lord and us.

Our whole family felt let down, but George was going through a difficult time, so we weren't about to give up on him. I continued to pray for him and tried to maintain contact every few months but kept our conversations on a superficial level. "Hey, I'm checking in to see how you're doing. How's business? Did you see the Jets game?" I felt led by the Holy Spirit not to push him about the Lord or to preach. It might trigger him and create more distance than was already there. My intention was to let George know we loved him and were there for him. This is the way it was for several years.

Time passed and one day in 2020 George called out of the blue to announce he was coming for a visit. We were so overjoyed to see him that we smothered him with hugs when he showed up at our front door. "I was driving, and I heard the voice of God very clearly telling me to make some changes in my life," George explained. "He also told me to come see you guys." As we rejoiced at our reunion, he thanked me for not being pushy and for just being a friend. I think the fact that I stayed in touch with him gave him reassurance he wasn't being abandoned. He told us the one constant he had was our family being there for him regardless of the turmoil in his life. Thankfully, George is walking with God again, and our friendship is stronger than ever.

Lessons in Loving and Helping Others

God has taught us some important lessons regarding trusting Him with our children and loved ones when they're going through difficult seasons.

Comparing children with their siblings or others outside the home is not God's way.

Each person is created by Him with a unique life blueprint for His purposes. Psalm 139:13–16 says:

> For You formed my inward parts; You covered me in my mother's womb. I will praise You, for I am fearfully and wonderfully made; marvelous are Your works, and that my soul knows very well. My frame was not hidden from You, when I was made in secret, and skillfully wrought in the lowest parts of the earth. Your eyes saw my substance, being yet unformed. And in Your book they all were written, the days fashioned for me, when as yet there were none of them.

God was intentional in the way He created us and ordained our days. Our job is to embrace our children's God-given differences and nurture the development of their gifts and talents.

It's important to show unconditional love by letting go of expectations, whether they are cultural or personal.

I'm learning to accept my children, family, and other loved ones at face value and try to remain steady and objective when their actions may be painful and they are difficult to deal with. Feeling disappointed is fruitless. All of us fall short, including myself. Peace comes when I understand it is what it is and get my focus off that person and onto the Lord for my hope and expectations. We can learn from the way Jesus showed unconditional love to a much despised tax collector named Zacchaeus in Luke 19.

When Zacchaeus heard that Jesus would be passing through his town, he wanted to catch a glimpse of Him, but because Zacchaeus was so short, the throng of people that had gathered along the road was blocking his view. Undeterred, Zacchaeus ran ahead of the crowd and climbed a sycamore tree. Jesus spotted him and said, "Zacchaeus, come down immediately. I must stay at your house today" (Luke 19:5, NIV). Jesus knew Zacchaeus' reputation, but that did not stop Him from engaging with the tax collector.

Meanwhile, the other people started murmuring because they couldn't stand the fact that Jesus had invited Himself to be a guest at the house of a sinner. Jesus showed unconditional love to Zacchaeus while the murmurers judged him for his actions instead of accepting him as a person while he was still in his current condition. Jesus' calling out to Zacchaeus had an immediate effect on the man, who said he would give away half his possessions to the poor and reimburse money to anyone he had cheated. As a result, Jesus said to him, "Today salvation has come to this house, because this man, too, is a son of Abraham. For the Son of Man came to seek and to save the lost" (Luke 19:9–10, NIV). We too are called to love people as Jesus did.

Learning that people think and process differently than I do helped me become more sympathetic.

Understanding this means considering other people's thoughts, feelings, and needs so we can adjust how we communicate and speak their language. Being sympathetic also involves being a good listener, being patient, and showing grace and mercy as people work out their issues. Paul told us that he had become all things to all people so that by all possible means he might save some (1 Cor. 9:22). He also encouraged us, "As the elect of God, holy and beloved, put on tender mercies, kindness, humility, meekness, longsuffering; bearing with one another, and forgiving one another, if anyone has a complaint against another; even as Christ forgave you, so you also must do. But above all these things put on love, which is the bond of perfection" (Col. 3:12–14).

Sometimes the Holy Spirit leads us to refrain from speaking, even if we think we know the answer, to stay out of God's way or allow the person to come to his or her own conclusion.

The Bible tells us we are to be quick to hear and slow to speak and our speech should be filled with grace and seasoned with salt (Jas. 1:19–20; Col. 4:6). Salt is used to preserve food and make it appetizing. So our speech should be. (See Proverbs 15:1 and Psalm 141:3.)

There is a blessing in moving forward with what God wants us to do, even if we don't see the present value in it or understand His ways.

In the beginning I didn't wholeheartedly embrace the idea of Daniel moving back home, but in the end God's purposes became clear. During that season, the Lord made the following scriptures real to me in a new and practical way: "Trust in the Lord with all your heart, and lean not on your own understanding; in all your ways acknowledge

Him, and He shall direct your paths" (Prov. 3:5–6). "'For My thoughts are not your thoughts, nor are your ways My ways,' says the LORD. 'For as the heavens are higher than the earth, so are My ways higher than your ways, and My thoughts than your thoughts'" (Isa. 55:8–9).

Pray bold, specific prayers, and claim God's promises.

Vicki and I prayed our son home! We also prayed about specific details concerning him and our friend George—deliverance from bad influences, people, situations, temptations, pride, rebellion, stubbornness, and so on. We prayed about every detail we were aware of and then made bold declarations from Scripture, speaking the scriptures out loud to God. We declared verses such as John 10:28–29: "And I give them eternal life, and they shall never perish; neither shall anyone snatch them out of My hand. My Father, who has given them to Me, is greater than all; and no one is able to snatch them out of My Father's hand." We also prayed scriptures such as Proverbs 22:6, Acts 16:31, and Romans 2:4.

Humility is key.

As I've said before, when pride rises up, it blocks the flow of the Spirit. I had to humble myself and ask for forgiveness to mend the relationship and regain trust with my son. I had to take seriously Paul's words in Philippians 2:3–4: "Let nothing be done through selfish ambition or conceit, but in lowliness of mind let each esteem others better than himself. Let each of you look out not only for his own interests, but also for the interests of others."

Setting Boundaries

I would be remiss if I did not touch on the importance of setting healthy boundaries. The Bible clearly commands us to help those in need. A beautiful promise comes to us in Isaiah that says,

> And if you spend yourselves in behalf of the hungry and satisfy the needs of the oppressed, then your light will rise in the darkness, and your night will become like the noonday. The Lord will guide you always; he will satisfy your needs in a sun-scorched land and will strengthen your frame. You will be like a well-watered garden, like a spring whose waters never fail.
>
> —Isaiah 58:10–11, niv

Clearly we are blessed when we give of ourselves on behalf of others. However, the Bible also shows us that we need limits and boundaries for our own protection and to protect our families. It takes wisdom and discernment to determine when we are being manipulated or in harm's way. For example, 1 Timothy 5:8 says, "Anyone who does not provide for their relatives, and especially for their own household, has denied the faith and is worse than an unbeliever" (niv). This speaks not only of physical provision but also of spiritual provision and protection.

We must guard our families. Think of it as pulling up the drawbridge, not burning the bridge. Vicki and I have faced some ugly situations involving family members, situations that taught us to always pray about whom God wants us to help, how to help, and how long to help. When the Holy Spirit directs us to help someone, we give generously of our time and resources. But when He says no, we obey without fear of condemnation from God or others, bearing in mind the words of Paul: "There is therefore now no condemnation to those who are in Christ Jesus, who do not walk according to the flesh, but according to the Spirit" (Rom. 8:1).

My brother, who is deceased, was a drug addict most of his life. I stayed in contact with him and helped him financially for a period of time when he lived in a halfway house. When he insisted on living with me, I told him no, and he started to threaten me by saying, "I'm going to find you and kill you." Even though he was my brother and my father was pressuring me to take him in, I had to make the hard decision to stop communicating with him to protect myself and my family. Relatives have also tried to make us feel guilty or shame us into helping them, particularly with unreasonable requests for money, by saying, "We're family," or, "What do you mean you won't help your own family?" We had to seek the Lord's wisdom and discern when to assist and when to say no.

Other relatives who lived with us sowed discord in our home until we set clear boundaries. This ruffled some feathers, but it was necessary for the well-being of our family and building of healthy relationships. The same principles hold true regarding helping people outside your family. The Book of Proverbs teaches us not to overstep boundaries and not to feel obligated to engage with everyone we meet. It says, "Let your foot be seldom in your neighbor's house, otherwise the neighbor will become weary of you and hate you" (Prov. 25:17, NRSV). And it says, "Do not answer a fool according to his folly, lest you also be like him" (Prov. 26:4).

The bottom line is, do not lose hope in helping your loved one get back on track with God. Commit him or her to God in constant prayer, and ask the Holy Spirit to guide you in what to say and do. When helping someone, you may find that you also need an adjustment, not only the person you are helping. Clearly my son had issues, but I had to be willing to change too. God is growing them, but He's also growing us.

Chapter 7

Staying Connected

IT'S TRUE WHAT they say, that behind every successful man is an even better woman. I've learned this fact full well. Another thing I've learned along my journey is while I have a prophetic gift, God most definitely speaks to me through my wife. In fact, God had to show me that my relationship with Vicki and how I handled my home were at the foundation of a fruitful ministry. It wasn't until my marriage and family were in order that God released my prophetic gift to the next level. There were things He needed to do in both me and Vicki for that foundation to be secure. If you are single, please don't dismiss this chapter as irrelevant. Often, having order in your significant relationships is a key that unlocks the doors to the next level in ministry.

There is no way my ministry life could have moved forward as it has without Vicki. She has been by my side the whole way, helping me navigate through all the personal issues, growing pains, and critical decisions we have faced while walking this ministry out. Not only did Vicki help by giving her emotional support, unique insight, and gift of faith, but she has helped me in practical ways when I've been gone by taking care of things with the kids and the house and assisting with my business. Yet more than appreciating her help in ministry, I truly know there is no way I could be at this point in my walk with God in general without Vicki. The Lord has used her countless times as His vessel to teach me more about Him. Truth be told, after thirty-two years of marriage, we have had a lot of ups and downs, yet God's grace has worked in both of us, growing us and using us to teach each other. I'm a better man because of Vicki, and she says she's a better woman because of me.

Early in our marriage, however, things got pretty rocky at times. There were even moments when I thought I might lose her. Most of our issues stemmed from ineffective communication and past insecurities. Vicki was growing spiritually at a faster pace than I was, and she had more faith. She knew we were unequally yoked and finally challenged me to step up and take my proper place as the head of the family, the way Scripture teaches. For some reason, even though I knew we had issues, I was content having things stay as they were. I thought, "Why change?" Vicki's response was to ask me to pray about it, and she committed to praying for me. She realized she couldn't nag me or push me into my role. She had to just be quiet and pray that God would talk to me and that I would listen. She must have known something, because as life moved forward, the Lord began drawing me closer to Him and speaking to me about being the man, husband, and father He created me to be. As I began to grow into my biblical role as the leader, Vicki was challenged to stay silent and trust God as He developed me, even if she did not agree with certain things I did.

As I mentioned in an earlier chapter, God has been faithful to put some great spiritual mentors in my life. I looked for older men who were spiritually mature and had experienced success in all fields, including marriage, since I wanted mine to last because my parents' marriage didn't. One such mentor was Jack Forde. He had a significant impact on my life in so many ways, particularly when it came to me communicating with Vicki more effectively and being the husband God called me to be.

One day Jack pointed out to me the difference in how Adam and Eve were made. "And the LORD God formed man of the dust of the ground, and breathed into his nostrils the breath of life; and man became a living being" (Gen. 2:7). So Adam was made from dirt. It's pretty basic and simple. Men usually think in simple terms, he explained to me. Adam was in charge of the garden before Eve, so he was alone when he was trying to solve problems. Men usually want to be alone and think about situations. It is how we are wired to process issues. "But for Adam no suitable helper was found. So the LORD God caused the man to fall into a deep sleep; and while he was sleeping, he took one of the man's ribs and then closed up the place with flesh. Then the Lord God made a woman from the rib he had taken out of the man, and he brought her to the man" (Gen. 2:20–22, NIV).

Eve was made from the rib of Adam, and Scripture says God brought Eve to Adam, meaning He brought Eve from somewhere. It does not say where, but since the man and woman were created differently, they can't possibly be the same. Once Jack taught me this, I started to think about all the arguments Vicki and I have had. A lot of them were because I wanted to navigate the issues on my own and not include her in the decision-making process. I would go to a quiet place, think about the situation, and come up with a solution. I would then tell Vicki what we were going to do.

I also saw something else in Genesis regarding the order of my household. "The Lord God took the man and put him in the Garden of Eden to work it and take care of it" (Gen. 2:15, NIV). So Adam first had a job, and then the Lord gave him a helpmate in Eve. How interesting is that? Adam had an assignment before God brought him Eve. Now keep following me here. Later in Genesis, when the serpent tempted Eve, Scripture says, "When the woman saw that the fruit of the tree was good for food and pleasing to the eye, and also desirable for gaining wisdom, she took some and ate it" (Gen. 3:6, NIV).

Notice that when Eve ate the fruit, nothing happened.

"She also gave some to her husband, who was with her, and he ate it. Then the eyes of both of them were opened, and they realized they were naked; so they sewed fig leaves together and made coverings for themselves" (Gen. 3:6–7, NIV). It was when Adam ate the fruit that their eyes were opened. This brought clarity to me that my place in the family is to be the head of the household. But what did that look like? As the Holy Spirit dealt with me and taught me, and Jack instructed me, I found out that it looks different than I thought—certainly different from the religious stereotypes of a dictator-like head of household.

Jack encouraged me to realize that while yes, I am the head of the household, that means it's my responsibility to love my wife, listen to her, and nurture her. Being a Christlike husband means building my wife up and becoming a servant leader. Doing so builds trust, and Vicki responds by respecting me and acknowledging me in my role. Now Vicki observes how I handle situations. She prays for me and offers advice. We are equally important to God and to each other. We simply have different roles. It's been said that Eve was taken from the rib of Adam, his side, to be by his side. The two become one flesh.

I have had to grow into my role as a husband, and I have made some mistakes along the way. One example is a time when my father was demanding to use my credit card. I felt an obligation to be a good, loyal son and let him use it. Vicki and I had an explosive argument over it because she did not agree with that decision. With us both having strong-willed personalities, we didn't talk for almost two weeks. It was a traumatic time, but when I calmed down, got still, and began to listen to the Holy Spirit, I heard Him whisper, "Vicki is right." Ultimately I obeyed, took Vicki's advice, and did not give my father the card. My dad didn't take it too well, but it was the right thing to do. Often, doing the right thing isn't popular. I wanted to just give in to my father, who was being unreasonable. Vicki saw through it, and though our decision was painful, without her reinforcement I would have plowed ahead and made a financial mistake.

As the leader of our home, I must include Vicki in the decision-making process. She has a different perspective than mine, and it is always wise to get her point of view when making critical decisions. Leaving your spouse out of the loop is never good for the relationship. To honor them, we need to understand how our spouses communicate. As I learned to communicate with Vicki, I came to understand that she is a verbal processor, meaning as we are talking, she's processing the situation, thinking it through, which is the opposite of how I process. I internalize. Everybody processes information differently, and part of truly loving and becoming one with your spouse is taking the time to understand the way he or she communicates.

After Vicki and I learned how we each work through challenges, we set up two simple ground rules that changed everything and brought peace to our communication process. Basically, when I need to think about a situation, I will have time to be alone to process. After I am done, Vicki and I come together, where she can verbally process the situation and we can determine what we are to do. It's that simple and very effective. It's all about intentionality and thoughtful consideration. As our communication skills were fortified and I grew into my role, our marriage soared to another level, which helped lay a solid foundation for our ministry. If our marriage relationship isn't good, then there's no way the ministry partnership can be strong.

Leading by Following God

I take my role as husband and father seriously, so when the speaking engagements started to come and the Lord led me to accept them, I knew some adjustments would need to be made. Traveling and being away from home was quite difficult at the beginning. When the day approached for me to leave, I would already start missing my family! And it seemed as though no matter how hard I tried to have things in order before I left, there was always something tumultuous going on that needed my attention. I had to learn to trust the Lord and Vicki.

As I wrote in my previous book, when Vicki was pregnant with our fourth child, we were anxious because we had lost the previous baby due to a miscarriage. Losing the baby crushed me emotionally and spiritually and was one of the lowest points in my walk with God. My faith was shaken to the core during this time because I had been trying my best to obediently please God, and honestly I felt He had let us down. About three months after the miscarriage, just as I was getting back on my feet spiritually, we were caught completely off guard when Vicki discovered she was pregnant again. We were extremely concerned about another miscarriage happening and for Vicki's health because the doctor had given us a strict warning to wait at least six months for Vicki's body to recover. We just couldn't go through another miscarriage, and God forbid something should happen to Vicki. I could feel my faith beginning to wobble again.

About four months into her pregnancy, I was asked to help with event production for a Christian outreach called Jammin' Against the Darkness. The organization is headed by Pastor Steve Jamison and is a unique youth revival outreach that combines top NBA players, Grammy Award–winning musicians, and compelling speakers. These events fill large sports arenas in cities across the country, with tens of thousands of youths in attendance. During the day there's a Jamfest outside the arenas featuring Christian artists and activities such as three-on-three basketball tournaments, BMX and skateboard demonstrations, and kids' entertainment. The main events in the evening are a huge concert, testimonials from NBA players, and basketball, bike, and skateboard demonstrations.[2] After the concert Pastor Steve gives a short message and then an altar call. The Holy Spirit led me to join the organization a few years prior, and I loved the people and the way they managed the event and finances with integrity.

This time the event was going to be held in Columbus, Ohio. I was planning on taking Sara and Daniel, who were nine and eight, respectively, at the time, so they would get experience helping people and could also see this kind of ministry in action. Our third child, Krissy, was two years old, so she would stay home with Vicki. As the time drew near for us to fly out, Vicki started experiencing some alarming symptoms. I kept a close watch on her and was ready to help out at a moment's notice. Again, I was on high alert.

On the night before we were to leave for Columbus, Vicki started having cramps, followed by bleeding. Light spotting was exactly what had happened with the miscarriage. My fear level went from zero to ten, as I couldn't believe this was happening again. Then depression hit me, as all I could think about was losing our baby and my poor wife. As the minutes passed like hours, Vicki continued to feel worse.

I called Pastor Steve and told him I may not come due to Vicki not feeling well. He fully understood and said I should stay home and not think about going to Columbus. They could get my job covered, so it would not be an issue. The right place for me was by my wife's side. I told Vicki I was going to cancel the trip and we would stay home in case things got worse. I needed to be around in case she had to go to the hospital, but I tried to keep myself busy instead of just hanging out by her bedside, making her nervous. Vicki was upstairs resting, and the more the night went on, the more restless I became. I had no peace and could only think about losing another child and something happening to Vicki. God seemed light-years away, and the anxiety kept building into a full-fledged panic.

I went into my office and tried to work to take my mind off things, but it was no use. Nothing worked. I kept asking Vicki if she needed anything, and she kept saying no. Clearly she was handling the situation better than I was. I called a few trusted friends and asked them to pray, but instead of me feeling peace, my anxiety grew! Then I took a pause, and when I did, my mentor friend Jack popped into my head. Vivid memories of him pacing the floor in circles, praying, played in my mind, so I started to pace around the house and pray. The more I prayed, the more my fear and anxiety decreased. I kept pacing and praying.

After checking in on Vicki and finding her feeling OK, I got the kids ready for bed. As I put the kids down to sleep, we prayed, and Sara asked, "If Mommy is sick, are we still going to Ohio?"

I said, "Probably not, but we'll see."

"Is Mommy going to be OK?" Daniel asked.

"Yes," I said, "she'll be fine." But I kept praying because it was the only thing keeping me at peace. After the kids were asleep, I kept praying in the silent house. As I paced and prayed, a strange thought popped into my head. "You need to go to Columbus." I stopped and thought, "What?

Where did that come from?" I ignored it and kept on praying, and the thought came again. At this point, I had made up my mind to stay home, and there was no way I could even think about leaving Vicki by herself, let alone with Krissy, who was a toddler.

It was getting late, and when I went upstairs, Vicki was up. I told her I put the kids to sleep and asked how she was feeling. She said she wasn't feeling well. I told her I was going to stay home to be with her. She told me that she had called her grandmother, and she would come in the morning to help out. I said OK and then washed up for bed. I tried to sleep, but the thought of going to Columbus kept invading my mind. I continued to counter that with, "No, I'm the head of this family, and I must stay home." But the thought kept coming back. I wrestled with the thought all night long. When morning came, I'd hardly had any sleep and was exhausted. While in the bathroom splashing water on my face, the thought of going to Columbus kept coming up but in a more intense way. "Lord," I prayed, "if this is You, then please grant me peace."

At that moment, a sudden peace fell over me. As the peace came over me, I said, "OK, if You want me to go, I will, but how am I going to tell Vicki at a time like this?" Now I was getting nervous in a different way. I knew God's voice but rarely used the phrase "God told me to do this" to Vicki, or anyone. This was going to be a true test if it was really Him speaking. I came out of the bathroom and went up to her while she was still in bed. I said, "Honey, I have something to tell you." She looked up at me, and I could see the exhaustion on her face. I said, "I am not sure how I can say this, but for some reason the Lord wants me to go to Columbus."

I was prepared for the worst when she said, "Yes, I know; the Lord told me you have to go."

"You sure?" I replied. "You're still spotting, and Krissy will need attention."

"I am sure," she said. "Besides, Grandma is coming, and everything will be fine."

I immediately started to pack for Sara, Daniel, and myself and then woke them up. The first thing they wanted to know was whether Mommy was OK. I assured them she was, even though I was still concerned. Reluctantly, the three of us left the house because I was being obedient. As we boarded the plane, thoughts of Vicki and losing another baby filled my mind. "How can I be away from her at a time like this?" I thought. We landed a few hours later, but I could not focus on my ministry job because I was so worried about what was going on back home and how I had left Vicki. We arrived at the hotel and got settled, and I called Vicki. She said she was feeling better and that the bleeding had stopped a short time after we left. I let out a big sigh of relief.

As the Jammin' Against the Darkness outreach unfolded and we did our ministry, it became evident why I had come and why Sara and Daniel had to take the trip. Sara witnessed event production work and was able to help out when she was called upon. This was her first exposure, and it had a profound influence on her future choices. She would eventually do production work in college and for a ministry school, where she now works full-time. Similarly, Daniel saw the audio and visual side of the show firsthand, how it was set up and executed. This is currently what he is studying in college and what he does for a living.

While I was at the event, I was pulled in many directions. I constantly carried two mobile phones—one for my work as a CFO and the other for event production logistics. I was constantly juggling between the two. It was difficult to stay focused between the two, and it seemed I had to keep choosing which was more important throughout the day. Little did I realize at the time, this trip was monumental in preparing us for major changes in our lives a few months later. Vicki understood this was a test of faith, and she learned to trust God regardless of what the circumstances looked like. She knew she'd heard from the Holy Spirit that I was supposed to go on the trip and had a supernatural peace that the unborn baby would be fine.

Things went smoothly once I left for the trip to Ohio, but that's not always the case. Sometimes when you're following God, things don't go so smoothly. A few years ago I was in Adelaide, Australia, for a speaking engagement. The trip was going well as far as ministering goes, but I was getting homesick and still had a few days left. The people were great, and everything was going along without a hitch until one particular day. I was getting ready to go onstage when my cell phone rang. It was Vicki. I thought it strange that she would be calling, because she usually texted me when I was doing ministry and waited for me to call her when I could. There was also a significant time difference, so I immediately answered. Her voice sounded panicky.

I said, "Is something wrong, honey?"

"I'm at church with Krissy, Paul, and Michael," she said. "I was bringing Krissy to a youth group, and she started to feel nauseated in the car. Then she started to feel dizzy and very hot."

"How is she now?" I asked.

"She's having trouble breathing," Vicki said. "She also feels faint and looks like she might pass out."

As Vicki was telling me this, my stomach began knotting up. I tried to remain calm, but all I could think about was being halfway across the world while my daughter was sick. I felt totally helpless. I told Vicki to call an ambulance right away since it seemed as if she might be going into shock. Tears filled my eyes as I ended the call. I immediately went into the bathroom to pray, "Lord, I need to go onstage now, but I am not settled. How am I supposed to minister with my child having breathing issues? I shouldn't have come. I should be home taking care of things."

As I started to get more emotional, I paused and said, "Lord, we had a deal. You take care of my family, and I do what You want me to do. I'm just reminding You of it. I know You are faithful to Your word, so please show me You have this under control." I walked out of the bathroom totally unsettled and went to my seat to mentally prepare myself to go on. For the rest of the time I was in my chair, I kept checking my phone for an update text, but nothing came. It was time for me to start, so I got up, and as I was walking to the stage, I got a text from Vicki. She said Krissy was in the emergency room and they were running tests. Now I started to get calm again. At least she was in the hospital, so if she needed care, they could help her.

I went up on the stage praying, and as I walked toward the middle of the stage, I felt a peace come over me that I can't describe. All I can tell you is I knew beyond a shadow of a doubt that Krissy was going to be OK. As I was ministering, I just had this amazing peace, and two hours flew by very quickly. As soon as I finished, I checked my phone, and Vicki had texted a few minutes before. The hospital was going to release Krissy. All the tests were normal, and they weren't really sure what had happened. They were in the process of discharging her and sending her home. Although we had to walk through this trauma, God still showed up for us and let us know He was there.

The Relationship Between Marriage and Ministry

If my household were not in order, I would never feel stable when I'm out doing ministry. Not having spiritual and material needs met creates instability for a family and is a distraction when ministering. If my family members are fighting or obligations aren't met before helping others,

I'd be a hypocrite. How could I go out and minister to people about relationships or the home if mine was falling apart? God's order is intimacy with Him first, then ministry to our family, followed by ministry to others, and lastly our work. As I reflect on the last thirty years of my life, I see how God has worked in phases to establish His order in my marriage and ministry.

God began by establishing a strong foundation in our marriage, and then He built my prophetic ministry over time as He continued perfecting our marriage relationship. The Lord called me, as the head of the household, into ministry first, and then He called Vicki. It wasn't because she was less important; rather, God needed to train me in the "field" so I could support Vicki and be an example to her. God also sent Vicki on her own assignments to develop her spiritual gifts. While we still do have individual ministry assignments, Vicki and I are now mature enough in our relationship and the development of our own spiritual gifts to minister alongside each other. We are partners in ministry. I am in awe of how God designed our relationship by bringing two very different individuals together in compatibility, balancing our marriage and ministry.

Vicki and I learned those lessons about trust, respect, decision-making, and communication early in our marriage, and while we disagreed over various things, it was truly the working of the Holy Spirit that we never disagreed on the decisions regarding accepting or rejecting ministry assignments. There needs to be agreement between a husband and wife on accepting ministry assignments. As I mentioned earlier, there is no ideal time for ministry. God can call on you during a busy time at work, when you're dealing with a health crisis, or some other time that seems inopportune. You need assurance that God has called you, and your spouse needs to be in agreement and included in the decision-making process. To do otherwise is acting out of God's divine order for marriage.

Excluding a spouse from the decision-making process, especially for major decisions, can cause resentment and bitterness. A lack of regular, deep, meaningful communication and of nurturing the relationship can chip away at the marriage, leading to a major breakdown. Issues do not resolve themselves if they are ignored or swept under the rug. They may be unseen for a while, but eventually they are going to seep into the open if not dealt with. When that happens, it's usually more painful. You must be intentional about preventing this from occurring. When marriage issues are not dealt with, they can lead to a deterioration of the relationship to the point that a couple live together as roommates instead of as husband and wife. This is not God's plan for any marriage, especially couples who are in ministry together. I have prayed for and counseled couples who have found themselves in this situation. Vicki and I believe our marriage relationship is our personal testimony to the world and that biblical marriage is a symbol of the following:

The love between Christ and His church

God's Word teaches husbands to love their wives as Christ loved the church and give himself up for her. Husbands should love their wives as their own bodies, nourishing and cherishing them, just as Christ does the church. Wives are taught to respect their husbands and submit to them in everything, as to the Lord. Scripture says:

> Husbands, love your wives, as Christ loved the church and gave himself up for her, that he might sanctify her, having cleansed her by the washing of water with the word, so that he might present the church to himself in splendor, without spot or wrinkle or any such thing, that she might be holy and without blemish. In the same way husbands should love their wives as their own bodies. He who loves his wife loves himself. For no one ever hated his own flesh, but nourishes and cherishes it, just as Christ does the church, because we are members of his body. "Therefore a man shall leave his father and mother and hold fast to his wife, and the two shall become one flesh." This mystery is profound, and I am saying that it refers to Christ and the church. However, let each one of you love his wife as himself, and let the wife see that she respects her husband.
>
> —Ephesians 5:25–33, esv

What have I learned about loving my wife?

- Be patient with her. Vicki and I process information differently; we have different temperaments and personalities. She has a different point of view. I had to learn to love and accept her as she went through her own phases in healing from past wounds. Even if I'm busy or it's not the best time or I don't feel like it, I make time to keep our communication open. This reinforces patience and understanding.
- Ensure she is seen, heard, and nurtured. I had to learn to be a good listener and hear Vicki out, even if her point of view was different from mine. This is vital in meeting her emotional needs by allowing her time to process what she is going through. She just needs me to listen to her. Early in our marriage we would get into arguments with voices raised because she felt she wasn't being heard or encouraged. I must admit, I wasn't completely tuned in and listening because, as the direct problem solver, I was too busy trying to give her the solutions and point out her errors instead of being sympathetic and showing her how much I cared in a way that she could understand and believe. I've had to learn to adjust my tone and choice of words because I love her and want to nurture and encourage her.

- Include her in the decision-making process, especially the major decisions. This will help your relationship to be grounded in mutual respect. We covered this, but it is worth mentioning again. I'll share the details about a situation, and we'll both pray individually and together about it. Then we come together and make a decision. We'll move forward only when we're both in agreement. We've learned that quick, individual decisions are usually not good ones. If I feel strongly that God is telling me to do something, Vicki would be willing to submit to my decision and trust the Lord to course correct if I make the wrong decision.

The hierarchy and order between Christ and His church

The Word of God says the husband is the head of the household as Christ is the head of the church: "Wives, submit to your own husbands, as to the Lord. For the husband is the head of the wife even as Christ is the head of the church, his body, and is himself its Savior. Now as the church submits to Christ, so also wives should submit in everything to their husbands" (Eph. 5:22–24, ESV). Again, the true understanding of this is the husband is not a dictator but one who loves his wife, as Christ loved the church and died for it.

If the household is in order, then everything is in order and the home is more comfortable to be in. As the leader of the family, I'm called to model Christ and create a safe, stable environment for Vicki and our children. They should not be living in fear but feel free to be themselves and make mistakes. As we are growing, we're going to make mistakes. When our kids make mistakes, we're going to talk about it, understand why they made the mistakes, and then learn from them and move forward. We make sure they repent and ask God for forgiveness first, assure them God will work things out, and then point out there are consequences to every decision. The way we put it is, "For such a smart kid that was an unwise decision." When there is grace in the home, it is more stable, and extending grace is really what God does with us.

I think it's interesting that the themes we've seen in this chapter—security, stability, creating a loving environment, grace, acceptance, being understood, and being seen and heard—are the elements that go into being a servant leader of the family like Jesus. The worldly idea is the head of household takes financial responsibility, and then he's done. That is certainly part of the equation, but that's not the only aspect. When you compare the financial needs with the emotional and spiritual needs, the emotional and spiritual needs of the family are much higher.

The union between God and His people as well as the relationship between a man and woman

In order for the marriage relationship to be harmonious, it must be in one accord. In Genesis we see the first illustration of the marriage partnership: "Therefore a man shall leave his father and mother and be joined to his wife, and they shall become one flesh" (Gen. 2:24). To me this means a husband and wife need to be on the same page, like-minded, and in one accord for family and ministry to flow. If we are not walking hand in hand in everything, we will be hindering the flow God has for us. God has brought Vicki and me to the point where we are not only physically connected but spiritually and emotionally connected. God brought Vicki to me. She's part of me, and I'm part of her. Together we are one flesh.

Vicki's Perspective in Her Own Words

I have shared about leading a marriage partnership from a husband's perspective, but I asked Vicki to share her wisdom from a wife's point of view. She too is called to ministry, and her willingness to obey God's instructions for wives has made it possible for us to be in sync in life and ministry. If wives who are called to ministry don't honor and respect their husbands, they will hinder the flow of the Holy Spirit in their lives.

> Let me begin with a little background. I entered into my marriage to Hubie with a lot of baggage. There had been a pattern of divorce, infidelity, and absentee fathers in my upbringing and family history. Then I discovered that my best friend's fiancé was openly cheating on her, which only added to my insecurity and reinforced my negative outlook on men and marriage. On top

of that I was raised in a non-affirming, highly critical atmosphere in which nothing I did was ever good enough. Any recognition of an achievement sounded like this: "Well, you did this, *but you didn't do...*" Thinking this was normal, I adopted this mindset as well. I became a controlling perfectionist who held myself and my husband to impossible standards, not knowing how unhealthy and damaging my behavior was to our relationship.

My first step in learning to respect and honor Hubie was becoming conscious of the critical spirit I was operating under. Early in our marriage Hubie would say, "I don't feel you're supporting me," and I felt hurt because I was clueless as to why he felt that way. I'm embarrassed to admit it, but I thought I was being helpful when I commented on things such as his clothing, appearance, and table manners and the volume of his speaking voice in a restaurant. Yet I was coming across as nitpicky, controlling, and condescending because I was being those things. I was so ashamed of myself after he repeatedly pointed these issues out to me. The Lord opened my eyes to this realization one day as I was grocery shopping. While walking through the meat section, looking for steak, I noticed an elderly man watching me examine and poke at the packs of steaks. He approached me and asked, "What are you doing there? How do you select the meat?"

I explained my process. "Oh," he responded as he looked at the pack of steak in his hand. "My wife sent me to get steak, and this is what I'm bringing back. She says I never do anything right." He shook his head sadly, crumpled the grocery list in his hand, and walked away. My heart broke for him because I could feel the pain of his dejection. And since he was an elderly man, I imagined he must have endured this type of ill treatment from his wife for decades. From that point on I knew I had to change my attitude and behavior. It did not come naturally to me to be positive and affirming, so many times I had to pause, bite my tongue, and check myself before I let a word come out of my mouth.

I am also called to model Christ by respecting Hubie, honoring him, and treating him the way I would want to be treated. The apostle Paul wrote in Philippians 2:3–4, "Do nothing from selfishness or empty conceit, but with humility consider one another as more important than yourselves; do not merely look out for your own personal interests, but also for the interests of others" (NASB). So I've learned to be intentional about the following:

- I give Hubie the grace and space to be the leader of our household. We agree most of the time; however, on the few occasions we disagree, we pray about the course of action, or I calmly submit to his decision, trusting God to course correct if necessary. I do not view submission as inferiority because I trust God's design for marriage. Ultimately my husband is accountable to God, and I know without a doubt his intention is to act in the best interest of his family.

- I regularly show Hubie appreciation by finding opportunities to compliment him on everyday tasks as well as bigger achievements. It's vitally important to let him know I see his efforts.
- If either of us makes a mistake, we calmly discuss it and gently provide correction, not criticism. Correction objectively identifies the mistake and provides a way forward. Criticism tears down and shames.
- I've learned to stop telling Hubie what to do—meaning nitpicking, nagging, or arguing with him about the small stuff. We each have our own way of doing things, and that's OK. Proverbs 21:9 warns about women who cause strife. "It is better to live on a corner of a roof than in a house shared with a contentious woman" (NASB). Instead, God instructs us to be peacemakers (Rom. 12:18).
- I avoid participating in the public humiliation of men by their wives or remove myself from the environment. I've been invited to church events and social gatherings with Christian couples at which the wives would gang up on their husbands and insult them to their faces. Then they would laugh about it with one another as their husbands sat quietly and avoided eye contact with people because they felt so embarrassed. A

> comment such as, "Why are you wearing that? I told you not to dress like that," or, "You see, I told him he should do this, but he won't listen to me," spoken in a derogatory tone in front of others is manipulative, demeaning, and hurtful. In these situations I get up and leave if I can, or if the opportunity arises, I rave about how wonderful my husband is, to try to redirect the conversation.

The way we handle relationships and our marriages and families is the foundation of fruitful ministry. If you are single, God wants to bring order and healing in the significant relationships in your life also, whether they are with family members, friends, or business or ministry partners. Until your relationships are in order, God cannot release your prophetic gift to the next level.

Chapter 8

When Things Go Wrong

WHAT DO YOU do when prophetic ministry goes wrong? How do you get your peace back and start again when you feel embarrassed and broken? Are there warning signs you can see beforehand so you can prepare yourself?

Not long ago I was invited to a presidential ball. It was a grand event with dignities, great food, music, and all the things that go along with an occasion like that. I felt honored to be invited. Sensing the Lord might have had a reason for me being there, I was open and pliable, listening to the Holy Spirit. Sure enough, a nudge came, and I was obedient. The recipient gave a neutral response and said thank you, but I wasn't discouraged. After that things took a nosedive. The night had hardly begun when it started turning into a nightmare. The second prophetic word I delivered was not well received at all. Let's just say the person didn't laugh and say, "Amazing," as SQuire and Louise did!

There were two women in the sitting area talking, and one appeared to be crying. Feeling prompted, I watched from a distance and waited until they were done, and then I went over and said hello to both women. Turning to the woman who appeared to be crying, I said, "I have something the Lord wants me to tell you." To my surprise the other woman responded with an annoyed voice, "Oh, you do?"

I nodded, and the first woman said, "Yes?"

After I gave her the word, she replied, "A lot of what you said was what this woman just told me, and you expanded on it and told me more." She thanked me and got up and left. I felt relieved that the message was accurate. Then the Lord told me to speak to the other woman, who had the attitude. This was *not* something I really wanted to do. I reluctantly sat down next to her and said, "The Lord wants to tell you something also."

Before I could start, she said, "Hold on a minute," and proceeded to use her cell phone to reply to texts and answer emails. At that point, I debated getting up and leaving but decided to be obedient and wait because that's what the Holy Spirit was leading me to do. After about five minutes, which seemed more like days, she said, "OK, I am ready now." I couldn't get over her attitude, but I put it aside and asked her if she wanted to record the prophetic word, and she asked, "Is it necessary?" I told her most people record the words because I don't know what I am saying and I usually cannot repeat it. She said, "Oh, hmm. OK."

The whole time I prophesied to her, she glared at me,

acting as if it was a complete waste of her time. When I finished, she said, "Are you done? I want to give you feedback."

"Sure," I responded, feeling a bit taken aback since no one I've prophesied to has ever offered to give me feedback. I know there is always more to learn, so I am open to it.

"When you give words," she instructed, "you need to tell more about what's coming rather than going back through my life from when I was younger because it's not relevant. I am so over all those things from my past, so you didn't need to bring those things up. You need to spend more time on the now and the future than going back to the past."

Stunned and confused by her negative response, I thought it was quite remarkable, seeing I hadn't known anything about her past. Nonetheless, I said, "OK," got up, and walked away. It was obvious something had gone wrong, and she was not happy about it.

Feeling like an idiot and a failure, I went back into the ballroom angry and annoyed. I no longer wanted to continue prophesying, even though the night was still young and there was a roomful of people who probably needed God's loving touch and affirmation. Sure enough, I felt the nudge to speak to another person. "No, God," I muttered. "I am done." The nudge stopped but came back later. The Holy Spirit is kind and gentle, and it was as if He was giving me some space. He must have poked me at least a dozen times, but I kept telling Him, "No more. I am done!" I just felt so angry and had no desire to continue. Sometimes I can be extreme, especially when I am upset.

Food service had begun, and I was hungry, but my stomach was churning so badly that I couldn't eat. As I mentioned in an earlier chapter, my stomach churning is one of my special signals from God that I need to speak to someone. It's quite unpleasant but has been a reliable indicator that God is calling me to an assignment. It starts with a feeling of unease and then progressively gets worse, to the point of nausea. The moment I tell Him yes, my stomach stops churning. Tonight, however, my self-absorbed emotions were allowing me to tune out everything, and I kept telling God no to the point that I felt so nauseated I wanted to throw up.

If I was serious about quitting, the Lord would have removed the nausea since I do have free will. It was clear I had a choice to make since I was getting really sick, so I decided to try one more time, and if that attempt didn't go well, I would leave for good. As I told the Lord yes, my stomach stopped churning and felt better.

The Lord told me to speak to a man sitting behind me. I turned around, glanced quickly, and turned back around. I waited a minute and then turned around again to tap him on the shoulder. The man turned around and said, "Hi, sonny." As he did, I recognized him as none other than Bill Hamon, a global leader in the prophetic movement. Of all the people in the room, why did it have to be him? The thought of giving a prophetic word to a major prophetic leader thoroughly intimidated me, especially since I was still trying to bounce back from the earlier incident with the woman correcting me on the prophecy she received. "What else could go wrong?" I mumbled to myself. "Oh, whatever; let's just get this over with." Obediently I told Bill Hamon I had a word for him.

"OK, sonny," he said and listened intently as the prophecy came forth. He nodded his head, affirming every point with an uh-huh. After I finished, he said, "OK, thank you very much. I appreciate it." That was it. He didn't seem blown away, but there was no sign of anything negative about it. I felt relieved, so I took that familiar deep breath and told the Lord OK, I would continue.

For everyone who is in prophetic ministry, it is only a matter of time before you give a prophetic word that is off or appears to be off until time proves it correct. For many of your words, people will not seem blown away, or they will show no emotion. This does not mean the prophetic word was off, but it can still shake your faith. Any of these situations can leave you with feelings of rejection and failure. No one wants to feel awkward and foolish in front of strangers or even in front of those who are familiar. When doing the Lord's work, those feelings are heightened because you don't want to fail God or look dumb. In my instance, unresolved rejection issues from my past affected my judgment, which is why I told God, "I'm done!"

Don't Give Up

So how do you move forward after something like this happens? When I was younger, my baseball coach taught me that if you mess up, pause, take a deep breath, and try it again, but take it little by little. Don't attempt too much too fast. Start with small steps, and gradually build your confidence back up, and then keep going forward. Vicki and I were in a terrible car accident once, and I had to force myself to get back in the car and drive so I would not lose my nerve. Another time, I almost drowned and knew if I didn't ease back into the water, I may never swim again. It's the same principle when moving in the prophetic. At the ball that night I made up my mind to trust God and take another step of faith, which is never easy.

Shortly after making that decision, my cell phone rang. It was Louise. She had called to check on me and see if I could meet her friends who were also at the president's ball. When she asked how I was doing, I told her what had happened with the woman, and she started to laugh uncontrollably. Again, as I did on our first call, I thought she was laughing at me, but she said, "No, no, no, no. Can you imagine the look on that woman's face one day when she turns on the TV and finds out who you are?" She thought it was hilarious, and I must admit, I thought it was funny too. Louise can always get me to smile and cheer me up.

That call made me feel better, and I continued to minister for another five to six hours, until around three o'clock in the morning. Sensing I had fulfilled my God assignment, I felt a peace fill my heart. As I was falling asleep that morning, the Holy Spirit whispered to me that the reason He had me speak to the woman with the attitude was He wanted to remind her of some things from her past that she hadn't really gotten over. The Holy Spirit was also reassuring me that I didn't mess up. This brought me comfort.

Another time, I went to church to pick up my daughter from the youth group. When I arrived, the Lord told me to speak to one of the pastors. The pastor said, "Hold on," and she continued to talk to other people and then checked her phone for messages, emails, and texts for at least five minutes. When I was finally speaking to her, she seemed super distracted instead of attentive. Frustrating me to no end, not only were her actions demeaning, but they made me feel as if I were wasting my time. When you tell someone you have a word from the Lord and the person says, "Oh, wait a minute," that's a sign that it may not go well. If God is important in the person's life, that person will stop whatever he or she is doing and listen. If you're going to give someone a prophetic word and the person puts you on hold for a long period of time, you should still be obedient and wait patiently but have your guard up because there is a chance it won't go well.

While attending a conference in Georgia with my mentor, Joseph Mattera, he asked me to prophesy to a man he had been ministering to. After I did, the man responded, "Oh," asked me for my number, and walked away. I later received an irate voice mail from that man, telling me I was "way off," and "as a matter of fact, it was so far from the truth." Feeling confused and upset at the possibility that I might have messed up, I talked to Joseph about what happened and shared with him the prophecy I had given this person. Joseph started laughing as he listened to the prophetic word and then told me that the word was accurate. In fact, the prophecy was so on point it had hit a nerve regarding issues this person was unwilling to deal with. His reaction was to attack the one who delivered the message, the very person who was trying to help him.

Don't expect people to always jump up and down with joy or applaud when you deliver a word from God to them. Being obedient doesn't necessarily mean the word will be accepted or received. Sometimes it stings them, and they will take it out on you. Prophecies are not all words that give goose bumps; sometimes they pinpoint hidden issues and strongholds in people's lives that God wants to heal and set them free of. They show that the Lord sees them in their circumstances, knows their name, and loves them. You must learn to put emotions aside and move forward despite feelings of inadequacy or anger. Becoming too emotional hinders your ability to focus on the assignment. Rejection can be extremely disheartening, but you can't take it personally, because the prophecy is not about you. Like a mail carrier, you are just delivering the mail—only the mail you are carrying happens to be a message from God.

You should not be affected one way or the other by validation or the lack thereof. Do not look for head nods, a thank-you, or an "I receive that." Again, it's not about you. As with the man in Georgia whom Joseph Mattera asked me to prophesy to, a prophecy may be rejected because its message hits a nerve and touches an issue a person is in denial about or unwilling to face. There will also always be naysayers and critics. Don't allow yourself to be distracted or discouraged by their remarks. Stay the course. The Lord is the One we strive to please. From Him comes our ultimate reward.

Authentic prophetic ministry is always initiated and led by the Holy Spirit. There is a not-so-glamorous side to prophesying, contrary to what is portrayed in modern-day religious culture, especially on social media, where prophetic ministers are placed on pedestals and "followed" as celebrities. You need to understand all aspects of authentic prophetic ministry to know what you're getting into. Obedience involves sacrifice and at times bearing the consequences of persecution and suffering. Throughout the Bible the prophets were persecuted. If you feel called to move in the prophetic, check your motives to make sure they are pure before God. Ask Him to give you confirmation before prophesying that the message is from Him and it is the right time to release the word. When I began in prophetic ministry, I did not want to make the mistake of prophesying in error, so I asked God for a sign. His answer was to make me feel sick!

Over the years, as I have dealt with things going wrong, or when I've perceived them to have gone wrong, the Lord has taught me not to rely on people's reactions. I do what I'm supposed to do, leave the results in His hands, and move on. I'm also learning that God is no respecter of status or title, nor is He a respecter of feelings when we are on assignment. Our job as prophetic voices is to lay aside our emotions and simply obey. Ezekiel 2:7 couldn't be plainer: "But speak My words to them whether they listen or refuse to listen" (HCSB). And Jeremiah 1:17 says, "Get yourself ready! Stand up and say to them whatever I command you. Do not be terrified by them, or I will terrify you before them" (NIV). That is sobering for all who desire to walk in the prophetic.

Remember, though, God is good, and it is His goodness that leads to repentance (Rom. 2:4). Second Timothy 1:7 says, "For God has not given us a spirit of fear and timidity, but of power, love, and self-discipline" (NLT). We can be firm and direct, but a spirit of love should always be behind our voices. God's ultimate purpose for prophetic words is to bring wholeness to the ones He is sending us to. The Holy Spirit is the Comforter, and He comforts. That night at the presidential ball, He comforted me at the end of the night with reassurance that I did not blow it with the woman who corrected me on the prophecy I gave her and that He was working in her life. If you have been faithful to deliver the word God gave you to give, He wants to comfort you when things seem to go wrong so you won't be discouraged and will keep moving forward in your gift.

When things go wrong, don't give up. Pause and listen to the Holy Spirit for insights and adjustments. Keep moving forward slowly, resting in the knowledge and confidence that He who called you is in control and the Holy Spirit inside you is guiding you. "Not that we are competent in ourselves to claim anything for ourselves, but our competence comes from God. He has made us competent as ministers of a new covenant" (2 Cor. 3:5–6, NIV). Remember, prophesying is not about impressing people but about getting His message out.

Chapter 9

When the Gift Goes Dormant

DURING THE COVID-19 pandemic the world shut down for a time and life as we knew it ceased. A new way of existing developed based on both a desire to protect ourselves and fear. Almost everyone had a friend, friend of a friend, or relative who died or nearly died of COVID-19. Staying home, avoiding crowds, social distancing, and masking became our reality. Politicians, educators, and medical experts were telling us this was our new normal. Whether we liked it or not, or agreed with it or not, all of us had to adjust. The lockdowns hit restaurants, theaters, small businesses, and churches the hardest. For me, speaking engagements got canceled and ministry opportunities dried up. What followed was months of being at home, away from everyone other than my immediate family. I ventured out of the house only to go grocery shopping or run errands. That was pretty much the extent of my traveling.

As time passed, I was surprised to discover how content I was staying at home and how much I enjoyed this new way of life. Blessed with the ability to work from home for most of 2020, I was completely fine not having to travel or be away from my family. I was also content not doing ministry outside the home because I understood that fellowship with the Lord and ministering to my wife and family were my first priorities. Being away on speaking engagements seemed far away.

Every now and then, however, questions would randomly pop into my mind regarding my prophetic gift and the fact that it wasn't being used. As the months lingered, the thoughts got more intense to where I started feeling anxiety and confusion. It brought me back to when the gift first started. The prophecies would come in spurts and then stop for a while and then come back. I didn't know if it was supposed to be systematic, consistent, or what. In the course of time, however, the gift became consistent. I also understood that some of the thoughts I was having were not my own. When I get this way, it has become my practice to get still, pray, and wait to hear from God.

By the summer of 2021, COVID-19 cases had leveled off somewhat, and society gradually started to open back up. My good friend pastor Walter Nistorenko of Abundant Life Church in Ocean View, New Jersey, called and asked if I could come to his church and minister to the students who attended his school of ministry. I took some time to pray about it, and when the Lord gave me the green light, I accepted the invitation. It had been quite a while since I had done a speaking engagement, and I knew that at some point I was going to have to take the plunge and get back out there. Prophetic ministry is all about being available and pliable. It is up to the Lord to lead, and it is *His* gift, so it is up to Him to turn it on and off. When the day arrived for the speaking engagement, I hopped into the car thinking I was in for a nice, relaxing drive to South Jersey.

The trip was going to take a few hours, so I was praying, as I usually do, when out of nowhere a fear gripped me and all those questions that popped in my head when I was shut in at home started bombarding my mind again. The more I tried to dismiss them, the more intense they became. One after another the questions kept coming, unnerving and unsettling me. Then a debate started in my head as I tried to reason and come up with answers. I was on my way to minister and didn't want to be carrying those lingering questions and be unsettled when I walked through the door. I've listed the questions and responses in this chapter to help you not only navigate your prophetic journey but also fully understand your spiritual DNA as God sees it.

Question: My gift is not being used. Does that mean something is wrong?

Answer: My gift was given to me to use at the Lord's discretion, so it is on loan. It is wrong to take ownership of it, because the Lord gave it to me to use when I am directed to use it, not when I want to or feel like I should. It is not part of my identity, and it does not define who I am. God is the One who triggers the gift, and I don't have to work or strive to earn His love. Instead, I can relax and move when He moves, resisting the temptation to rush or view times of quietness as a negative.

Again, I will be intentional and will not think of the gift as part of my identity because that's not what the Lord wants. I will use my gift for Him, not for myself. This takes the pressure off. For example, during the COVID-19 pandemic and the presidential election, people were calling and pressing me for a prophetic word. I was fine saying, "No, sorry. I don't have anything." If I try to do something in my own effort, it can be dangerous. The gift is a tool. When I am called to use it at the right time and place, I take it out of the toolbox and use it. When the job is done, I put it back until I am called to use it again.

Question: Am I doing something wrong that is hindering the gift?

Answer: I attempt to live in a state of self-examination, staying transparent and honest before the Lord and nurturing an intimate relationship with Him. I am not really concerned about something hindering my prophetic walk as long as I'm walking in consistent fellowship with the Lord. If I do not pray or stay connected, then this can become an issue.

Question: Is the gift gone?

Answer: Years ago, when the prophetic gift was first activated in me, it took me a while to get accustomed to it. I remember being at a friend's church, and one of the staff members and I were chatting. He saw I was having issues adjusting to ministry, and he asked me, "If you could ask the Lord to take the gift away, would you?" I remember pausing and telling him I would need to think about it. What concerns me now when I think back on that time is that I actually had to take time to think about it. I wasn't ready to simply accept that the Lord knows more than I do. He knows what my full purpose is and what will fulfill me.

The Bible says I am "His workmanship, created in Christ Jesus for good works, which God prepared beforehand that [I] should walk in them" (Eph. 2:10). At that time, however, I didn't fully understand my purpose or identity in Him. I knew I was saved but had not dealt with my insecurities and rejection issues. But now that healing has come, I've grown to the point that if the Lord wanted to take the gift away, I would miss it since I now know all the people it can help by giving them encouragement and direction. Prophecy is a powerful ministry tool when used correctly and biblically, but if God does take it away, I'm fine with that because the gift doesn't define me and I really don't have any ownership over it.

Question: Is something wrong with my faith?

Answer: Since the prophetic is activated by faith, this question especially bothered me and gave me anxiety. After what Vicki and I have walked through since this journey began, I don't think it would be possible to go back. We have gone through so many challenges, and God has been faithful through them all. Whenever my prophetic gift goes dormant, I increase my prayer and intercession, listening for the Holy Spirit's direction in other areas. Prophesying is not my only gift. When God makes it go silent, He often raises up other gifts that He has placed in me. Dormancy for a season gives me more time to concentrate on those other gifts. There are many good things we can unpack from the silence.

It's like when I couldn't play the guitar for over a year because of tendinitis in my elbows. I didn't stop doing guitar stuff. I continued tinkering with the tones with the guitar and in the process learned new things. If your gift goes dormant, don't try to force it to come back. God will bring it back at the right time. Learn to be yourself. It is a time of self-reflection. Maybe He's trying to draw you closer to Him. He longs for that fellowship. In the times when my gift was being rested, I was able to focus on other things God wanted to develop in me.

Question: Will my gift come back if I try to use it?

Answer: I couldn't really answer this question while I was driving, but I was going to find out shortly at Abundant

Life Church. The anxiety and uncertainty didn't stop me because I knew God was sending me.

When I arrived, Pastor Walter and his wife, Anna, who is also a pastor, greeted me. It was the first time I had been back in God's house since the pandemic started, so it was an emotional time. In Pastor Walter's office, we started to catch up on our families and life. Then the conversation turned to ministry.

"How long has it been since you ministered?" Pastor Walter asked.

"Not much since the pandemic started, so it has been a while," I said.

"Do you think you are rusty?"

"We will see," I nervously replied.

He let out a deep laugh. "This is going to be good!" he said as he rubbed his hands together.

Pastor Walter led me to the room where the students had gathered. I sat down before them and asked how everyone was doing. It had been a while since I had done this, so I was trying to get settled and was interceding the whole time, waiting for the Holy Spirit to help me. The easiest way for me to get into the flow is to ask everyone to also start praying. This settles everyone down and creates an atmosphere of expectation of the Holy Spirit to start moving.

When the praying subsided, I sensed it was time to speak but wasn't getting a specific leading from the Lord, so I updated everyone on what was going on with the ministry and my personal life. It was pretty scary not to have anything. I mean, everybody was there to see me, and they had expectations. I wait for the Holy Spirit to show up, and if He doesn't, it can be a very awkward situation. While I was talking, I kept interceding in my mind and waiting. Eventually the Lord faithfully began to lead me forward. Feeling relieved, I flowed in ministering to the students, and the next few hours were like a blur, but it was all good. God had shown up.

It's critical to point out here that if the Lord had given me nothing, I would not have moved forward. If nothing happens, nothing happens. I would rather disappoint a few people than misrepresent God and possibly hurt someone. The memory of Vicki and me being hurt by false prophecy is always in the back of my mind. The Lord leads, and I follow. It's as simple as that. If He doesn't lead, then I do nothing, even if it is embarrassing. To walk authentically in the prophetic and guard ourselves from false words, we must be willing to be embarrassed every now and then when obedience means saying nothing.

Early on in my ministry this was not always the case for me. I placed the responsibility on myself to have a word for everyone. When I didn't, I felt like a failure and that I was disappointing God. "What about that person who was truly seeking God and looking to me and I came up empty?" I'd think. "They were looking for direction from Him, and I couldn't help them move forward." As I look back now, I realize I was too focused on myself and my feelings instead of just letting God lead. This was an error. We can't take responsibility for God.

Throughout the years of my prophetic journey, people have put pressure on me to deliver words from God to them. I've finally been set free from the need to produce something that is not there, just to please people. I've heard all kinds of comments from people over the years:

- "I have traveled here to see and meet you. The Lord told me you had a word for me."
- "You don't have a word for me? Are you saying God doesn't love me?"
- "I have been searching for God for many years, and you are the closest I have come to actually knowing Him. Are you sure you do not have a prophetic word for me?"
- "Are you sure you aren't a con artist? Because all people can fake prophecy."
- "You prophesied to Jonathan Cahn, and you do not have a word for me? Am I not just as important?"

The answers to those questions vary, but they ultimately rest on God's sovereignty. He will always answer His children. In fact, He promises this in John 10:27: "My sheep hear My voice, and I know them, and they follow Me." This doesn't mean God won't provide a word of encouragement or direction, but it may not often follow the pattern the person desires.

One of the biggest lessons I have learned is to simply be myself. There's nothing to prove or feel pressured about. Silence and pauses can also be a test from God. Patience is the key. We must wait and listen, resting in Him. I am OK if God chooses to let the gift lie dormant for a season, or for a lifetime. Whenever I sense pressure to move forward or do something, I have discovered it's in my best interest to take a step back and pause. I reflect on those times when I rushed or pushed, and the results were negative most of the time. Those were costly lessons, but I am thankful for finally understanding.

I learned this principle one day while reading the biblical story of David at Ziklag, which is found in 1 Samuel 30. The story goes like this. David and his band of mighty warriors had been gone for several days doing what warriors do, and when they returned, they were shocked to find their hometown village of Ziklag burned to the ground and raided by the Amalekites. Worse, their wives, sons, and daughters had been taken captive. While the enemy didn't kill them, who knows what plans they had for them. The Scriptures say the men were so broken they wept until they had no more power to weep. Imagine these mighty warriors, these men's men, weeping until their strength was gone.

At that time, David's men surely were so overtaken with rage, pain, and grief that they wanted to chase down the Amalekites and save their families. They were probably expecting David to take charge and join them, but that is not what he did. Instead, David paused and went before the Lord to seek His guidance and encourage himself in God's presence. This wasn't the most popular move, but David was greatly distressed because of his own grief and the fact that his own men wanted to turn against him and stone him.

The pressure David was under is hard for us to imagine. He wanted to be the leader God anointed him to be and pursue the enemy, rescuing everyone's loved ones. In the physical sense that seemed like the right and obvious thing to do. But David wanted to be sure that's what God wanted them to do. So he sought God first and then waited while everyone else was eager to go after the enemy. Think of the courage it took for David to pause and seek the Lord in that situation. It's difficult to imagine myself in those shoes and what I would have done. Yet I'm convinced that if David could take a pause in that high-pressure situation, I can take a pause in almost any situation I face.

Look at how the Lord responded to David.

> So David inquired of the LORD, saying, "Shall I pursue this troop? Shall I overtake them?" And He answered him, "Pursue, for you shall surely overtake them and without fail recover all."
>
> —1 SAMUEL 30:8

That is exactly what David and his mighty men did! God honored David's pause. That's what God does. "The LORD is good to those who wait for Him, to the soul who seeks Him" (Lam. 3:25). And Scripture says, "But those who wait on the LORD shall renew their strength; they shall mount up with wings like eagles, they shall run and not be weary, they shall walk and not faint" (Isa. 40:31).

When my gift went silent, I was praying a lot, and although I felt uneasy doing nothing, I paused and listened and only moved forward as the Lord released me. When I think about the gift being His and not mine, it brings me comfort. It is His job and not mine to move it forward. I have also learned pausing is an effective way to self-reflect. It allows time to evaluate what the Lord is showing you and allows you to verify if you are supposed to deliver a prophetic word. Just because the Lord told you something doesn't mean it's to be shared. You have to check in with Him to see. Asking yourself the following questions can help you process: "Why did the Lord really show this to me? Was it to teach me how He speaks to me? Am I supposed to deliver it? Is it the right time for me to share, or should I wait?"

Timing in the prophetic is critical. Being too late or too early can create issues, but we can trust that God's timing is always perfect. We don't need to feel pressure, but we need to have an ear that is tuned in to His nudges to stay silent, speak now, or pause. Remember, you don't have to push or force anything. Even if the gift inside you is dormant, God is still working. Again, the Lord loves you, and your identity is Him, not your gift. Relax and just be yourself. Your gift makes room for you if you are in a quiet place seeking Him.

Chapter 10

Can God Trust You With the Prophetic?

I INTRODUCED YOU TO SQuire and Louise, authors of the Godwink series, in chapter 1. As my relationship with them developed, I got a nudge from the Holy Spirit that He had a message for their close friend, Kathie Lee Gifford. This made me nervous for several reasons. Whenever I sense a nudge like this, the first thought that goes through my mind is, "What could go wrong?" Being a CPA, I was taught to assume the worst, and that's how I usually approach situations. Far too often the prophetic gifting has been viewed negatively because someone followed their impulse rather than the leading of the Holy Spirit. So I approach any ministry opportunity with caution mixed with a bit of reluctance.

In this instance the only possible way I could think of to get the prophetic word to Kathie Lee was to ask SQuire and Louise to help deliver it to her. So the first and most obvious thing that could go wrong was I could come across as trying to manipulate my friendship with them to get to Kathie Lee for personal advancement. That is not who I am. I hate when people try to use me to advance their own agenda, and I make it a point not to ask for ministry favors. I didn't need anything to happen for me regarding Kathie Lee, nor did I want it to. But I knew the whole thing could backfire, and instead of ministering to Kathie Lee, I could push SQuire and Louise away. Or Kathie Lee could get offended, which would also damage my relationship with SQuire and Louise or cause issues between SQuire and Louise and Kathie Lee.

Understandably, most famous people keep boundaries for their protection because people are continually trying to get at them. All this was running through my mind and making me reluctant once again. Yet no matter how much I tried to avoid it, the nudge churned my stomach and grew stronger until I could hardly take it. Finally, I acknowledged this was not about me and set my reputation aside. "OK, Lord," I said, "I will do what You want."

Sometimes people hold back because they think being seen would make them look prideful. However, staying in the shadows when God says to step out is a type of pride because you're making it about you. At times, true humility means stepping out of hiding and exposing yourself to do what God has said to do. With this comes the possibility of criticism, missing it and looking like a fool, people perceiving you the wrong way, and so on. Pride in prophecy works two ways. It can be prideful to step out if you are doing it to be seen and promote yourself. It also can be prideful to hold back and stay hidden if you are doing so because of fear of what others may think. The true test either way is your heart's motive.

I was restless for a couple of nights, so I decided to reach out to SQuire and let him know I believed God was giving me a prophetic word for Kathie Lee. Other than knowing she was famous and on television, I knew little about her. I rarely watched television and had never even seen her on *Live! With Regis and Kathie Lee* or the *Today* show. I do remember seeing her on a show called *Name That Tune*. I texted SQuire and told him about the prophetic word I had for Kathie Lee. Wondering how I should send it to her, I asked, "Do you think you can help me get it to her? Do you think you can give me her email address?"

"As it so happens, Louise and I are actually having lunch with her now!" SQuire replied.

When SQuire said that, I knew instantly the Lord totally set me up, and His timing was perfect as always! I even told God that. Yet as I sat down at the computer to type out what He wanted to tell Kathie Lee, a flood of fear engulfed me and my hands started shaking intensely over the keys. "Lord, what is going on?" I thought. SQuire was waiting at the table with Louise and Kathie Lee, so I texted him, "I am getting sick and nervous."

"Don't worry," he replied. "Just send it. It will be OK," he reassured me.

After receiving those encouraging words from SQuire, I collected myself and tried to just let my fingers type whatever they needed to. When I finally finished, I attempted to read it, but my hands were still shaking so badly that it was difficult to concentrate. The fear of what could go wrong was getting worse. "Lord, I am just going to send it." I hit the send button, and off the email went to SQuire's email address. I texted SQuire that I had just sent it.

"Good!" he said. "When I get it, I will give her my phone so she can read it."

Negative thoughts filled my mind as I anxiously waited at my computer to see if I had just ruined a new friendship. Time passed so slowly that I got up and made a cup of coffee to distract myself. Several sips later, my cell phone dinged, indicating a text. It was SQuire. "Kathie Lee says thank you!"

I replied, "OK," because I wasn't sure what the message meant.

SQuire followed up a few minutes later to say she was encouraged and thankful. I breathed a huge sigh of relief. The prophetic word was on target, so I could now relax. In fact, Kathie Lee was so moved that she wanted to meet Vicki and me. This was the starting point of what would blossom into a wonderful and authentic friendship. Her trust in my prophetic gift and confidence that Vicki and I were not out to get anything from her allowed her to lower her boundaries for us. Just as it happened with SQuire and Louise, Jonathan Cahn, David Tyree, and others, Vicki and I learned so much about Jesus through

Kathie Lee and her life. Proverbs 27:17 tells us, "As iron sharpens iron, so one person sharpens another" (NIV).

This simply means that in God-ordained relationships, we bring different gifts to the table, and we make each other sharper and more effective. One thing I truly admire about Kathie Lee is whenever we talk, Jesus is always part of our conversation. She always brings up her scripture of the day, and she is very knowledgeable about the Bible. Vicki and I were surprised when Kathie Lee asked to interview me for her new book, *The Jesus I Know*. We were not looking for anything from her; we saw it as God's favor and an opportunity for further ministry.

For me, God bringing me before prominent people seems to be a pattern. I and most of my ministry friends marvel at how God keeps slipping me in the back door to meet people that an ordinary person like me would normally never cross paths with. It's not my intention to boast here but rather to relay an important element in effective prophecy. Paul was not boasting when he wrote, "Imitate me, just as I also imitate Christ" (1 Cor. 11:1). He was simply teaching by example and understood what he had learned. Likewise, I am merely relaying to you what I've learned. And one main point is this: integrity is key. Can God trust you with His prophetic gift? Will you take care of it, nurture it, and use it as you are supposed to? Remember, the gift is His, not yours. It is up to Him, not you, to direct.

I think God brings me before prominent people because He can trust me to use the prophetic gift the way it's supposed to be used. He truly knows I don't care about promoting myself or being associated with famous people; I am only interested in helping them know more about Him when *He* opens the doors for me to speak to them. In 1 Corinthians 14 Paul encourages everyone to pursue the gift of prophecy for the purpose of strengthening, encouraging, and comforting believers or bringing about conviction of sin to unbelievers who happen to be visiting the gathering of God's people "as the secrets of their hearts are laid bare" (1 Cor. 14:25, NIV). If you are promoting yourself, then how can He trust you?

This is a very serious thing. We can't misrepresent God. And be very careful about saying, "Thus says the Lord," when you prophesy, because that usually refers to Scripture that is already written. We are only stewards. The moment we begin feeling our own importance or start promoting ourselves, the Lord cannot trust us. It's that simple. Taking ownership of the prophetic gift for self-promotion or as your identity—in other words, making it *yours*—causes you to feel pressure to perform and lose your objectivity because instead of obeying the voice of the Holy Spirit, you might very well be deceived by the fleshly desires of your heart.

This is how the prophetic gift can be abused and become harmfully deceptive to the people receiving such "prophecies." When operating in the prophetic, we must remove self from the equation and be beyond careful. Jeremiah 17:9 tells us, "The heart is more deceitful than all else and is desperately sick; who can understand it?" (NASB). God wants to speak into people's lives, and He is searching for willing vessels to deliver His messages, those with pure motives who are open and pliable before Him.

Displaying integrity in prophetic ministry means being trustworthy and tight-lipped about those you are ministering to. They've let their guards down, which puts them in a vulnerable position. The prophecy might have revealed some issues of their hearts, or they might have asked for counsel and shared some personal information with you. No one wants to be exposed or gossiped about. And again, integrity means not being manipulative or taking advantage of others for your personal gain. Since God brings me before prominent people, for me, having integrity means not asking for favors or to get financial needs met. I don't make introductions or network. God is capable of opening doors and setting up divine appointments. It's His job, not mine.

Having to say no to people has caused issues at times, but unless the Lord specifically instructs me to make an introduction, I will not take part in it. If the Lord wants you to meet a certain person, then He will provide a way, as He did in the case of Jonathan Cahn, author of the best seller *The Harbinger*. Our job is to rest in Him and be available and obedient. The favor of God follows when you are being obedient and using the gift the right way. The opposite occurs when you promote yourself and use people. I know a man who had a large ministry with several wealthy board members. During prayer times he would drop hints about his financial needs. This became his pattern. People took note of his manipulation, and he eventually lost his whole ministry.

As you flow with the Holy Spirit in prophetic ministry, there are basically three types of people you meet and minister to: those you will never see again, those who will pop in and out of your life, and those you will become longtime friends or associates with. Sometimes the prophetic word is a one-off; other times there's a relationship. Either way there is a purpose in all meetings.

When God brings a person into my life, I don't know which category he or she will fall into. Since I don't know how long the assignment will be, I try to make myself available, again to just be pliable and open to the Holy Spirit. You can't go into an encounter with someone with expectations, because you don't know how long it's going to last. You can't get attached either. Don't let yourself get disappointed if a relationship doesn't develop. It's a mistake to try to force things. Trust me, you don't want someone in your life who is not supposed to be there; I don't care who they are. Make the most of the time and make yourself available to fulfill what God wants through the situation.

Some relationships flow in and out. You minister to a person when he is wounded; then that person goes on his way, and you fall out of touch. Then sometime later God brings him back into your life. This is different from a "do life together" community. I've had relationships over the years that seemed long-term, but we wound up going on separate paths. Time passed between us communicating, sometimes years, and then we finally reconnected. When we did, it was as if we never separated. I recently reconnected with a friend named Margie from when I was a teenager. As we started to catch up on things from all the years that passed, it was as though we had only spent a little time apart. We were still good friends and were picking up where we left off. My friendships with SQuire, Louise, and Kathie Lee are examples of divine appointments that evolved into authentic relationships. They developed over time as trust was built.

Keep Your Priorities in Order

When it comes to making ourselves available to God for His use, we must be careful not to neglect our family or use ministry as a means of escaping family issues. As I mentioned in an earlier chapter, our priorities should be intimacy with God first, then ministry to our family, then ministry to others, and lastly work—this is God's order. Personally, I am constantly busy with family and work and don't have a lot of time. I'm not in full-time ministry, so there's a lot of juggling of these four responsibilities. When God calls on me to minister to someone or take a ministry trip, it rarely comes at a convenient or ideal time, but it immediately becomes my top priority.

I've had to learn to trust Him by surrendering my to-do

list and tax deadlines, which at times puts a lot of pressure on me to finish my work once ministry is done. Despite this, God has been faithful over the years to sustain me and to meet every deadline, even down to the last seconds before the clock strikes midnight! "Cast your burden on the Lord," wrote the psalmist, "and He shall sustain you; He shall never permit the righteous to be moved" (Ps. 55:22). What a promise! When we are doing the Lord's will and work, we can depend on His faithfulness to take care of our needs, even when the need is meeting a work deadline!

I've encountered many people in ministry who do not have their families in order. They can't wait to get on the road because they don't want to deal with the issues at home with their spouse and kids. COVID-19 lockdowns put a stop to much of that and forced couples to be together and deal with issues they had been avoiding. There was tension in many relationships as a result of being shut in. Problems came to light, and divorce rates skyrocketed. Work and ministry can be distractions from what's most important. Personally I like to be home. Cooking, taking the kids to school, going to the grocery store, and doing things like that are a joy to me. The demands of traveling and ministering are not something I wanted or even desired, so I earnestly pray about every ministry invitation before responding instead of assuming every invitation is from the Lord. When the pandemic hit, I canceled all my trips and stayed home. I was happy spending quality time with my family, doing things around the house, and just being an accountant. I knew it would not stay this way, so I cherished each moment.

However, I need to be transparent in sharing that I did not always feel this way. Vicki and I had to learn some difficult lessons on getting our household into God's order. Early in our marriage we played the blame game whenever we argued because we felt disappointed that the other person did not meet our expectations. The same dynamic repeated itself with our children. It was always the other person's fault! So the long hours I worked during tax season or traveling became easy excuses for leaving issues unresolved. Vicki would raise her voice and yell, and then retreat to her home office when tensions boiled over. The less time we made available for our family, the more the relationships unraveled, so we had an unhappy home life.

One day I had a conversation about this with my close friend and mentor Jack Forde. Instead of lending a sympathetic ear, he dropped a bomb on me by saying that since I am the head of the household, the whole situation was my fault! I was so irritated by Jack's statement. I mean, how could this all be my fault when Vicki and the kids had their own issues? Jack went on to explain, "Marriage and family relationships are successful because of what you put into them, not what you feel you deserve or want from them." After Jack explained this to me, I understood his meaning, and I realized that our relationships with those we love are prophetic in nature. We often have to look past *what is* and see *what will be.*

Let me explain. The prophetic is often focused on a foretelling of things that will happen in the future. The prophecy can be given days, months, or even years before the events happen. But if God has declared it, that thing will come to pass. When something isn't going well in our homes or family lives, it's important to look at the issues with a prophetic eye and declare what it will be. It takes courage and conviction to hold on to God's Word despite the circumstances. Are you willing to take that step? It's difficult to do, as it is easy to lose hope when a situation seems impossible. God's Word is a lamp upon our feet, which means we may see only a few steps ahead. However, as we walk closely in obedience to God, we can rest in the knowledge that He will guide us step-by-step. God delights in doing the extraordinary. Our relationships are important to Him, and when God can trust us with His gifts, we can be sure those relationships will be redeemed.

For the prophetic gift to flow through us, God must be able to trust us. We must guard our hearts against the temptation to manipulate God's spiritual gifts for our own advancement. The long-term outcome of relationships with people we minister to is up to God, not us. Our role is to embrace these relationships loosely, letting them go if that is His will. Our priorities need to be in order—intimacy with God, ministry to family, ministry to others, and then work. When our priorities are in order, we can trust Him to repair our family relationships. If God can trust us, then there is no limit to what He can do with us!

Conclusion

As I've mentioned, walking with the Lord as a prophetic minister hasn't been easy, nor is it filled with notoriety and glamour. Stepping out in faith to speak with a total stranger is hard. You never know how a person will react, so your trust must be grounded in the knowledge that God has sent you. Your focus must be on the mission at hand rather than the person's facial expression.

The principles in each of the chapters will help you avoid the prophetic pitfalls that could sideline you from walking in the fullness of your gifting. So let's recap:

- God initiates the divine appointments.
- Prophetic ministers must die to themselves.
- Your gift is not your identity.
- Be comfortable in your own skin.

- Have integrity—don't manipulate people or your gifting.
- Deal with your personal issues.
- Get your priorities in God's order: God, family, ministry, then work.
- Solid relationships are the foundation of a fruitful ministry and life.
- Your gift will make room for you—platforms and notoriety are important to man but not to God.

Once these principles have become part of your life, you'll see the blessings of the prophetic. It's a powerful gift that can bring comfort, activation, and even answers in a personal way. God is always looking for pure vessels through whom He can demonstrate His love and reveal His perspective to those seeking Him. Are you willing to accept the challenge?

Surely the Sovereign Lord does nothing without revealing his plan to his servants the prophets.

—Amos 3:7, NIV

Notes

Chapter 1

1. Facebook direct message to author, March 22, 2014.

Chapter 7

2. "Jammin' Against the Darkness," Facebook, accessed January 10, 2022, https://www.facebook.com/jamminevents/.